A Hundred
Wild
Things

A Field Guide to Plants in the
Greenbelt North Woods

Owen A. Kelley

The author may be contacted at okelley@gmu.edu
and at 15 Lakeside Drive, Greenbelt, MD 20770. The
photos and text are the work of the author. Printed
in the USA. Front cover and title page: Tulip poplar
leaf. Inset photos clockwise from upper left are fan
clubmoss, sweetgum seed pod, wine raspberry branch,
and flower of flowering dogwood. Back cover: Waxy
cap mushroom and Indian cucumber root flower.

ISBN: 978-0-9670633-3-1

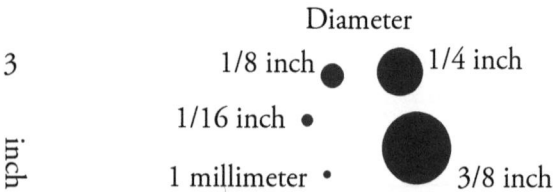

Diameter

1/8 inch ● ● 1/4 inch

1/16 inch ●

1 millimeter · ● 3/8 inch

Warning: When walking in Maryland's forests, take
precautions against ticks and know how to identify
poison ivy. Do not pick flowers or otherwise damage
plants in the Greenbelt Forest Preserve because
such actions are punishable by fines according to
City Code. Berries and other parts of plants may
be poisonous, so do not eat them or let your pet eat
them. As Rhea Cohen, a Greenbelt environmentalist,
wrote in 1985: the forest demands respect from those
who visit it.

Contents

Dear Reader — In 2015, the City of Greenbelt hired a consulting company to evaluate the health of the North Woods. I felt ill-prepared to weigh the merits of whatever report the company would produce. Like a number of other Greenbelt residents, I felt fiercely protective of this forest's wild character, so I decided to take a walk in the forest. Many walks. I photographed anything that caught my eye, and I asked for help in identifying what the camera saw. I wanted to share these wild shapes—leaf, bud, flower, and fungus—so I turned my photo collection into the book you are holding.

The North Woods, like the rest of Old Greenbelt, owes its existence to government efforts to reduce suffering during the Great Depression. Roosevelt's New Deal conceived of Greenbelt to demonstrate of the benefits of town planning. It was a whole town engineered to be a healthy place to live. Cooperative ownership was central to the experiment, as was a permanent belt of forest, field, and other green space.

Invoking the New Deal plan for Greenbelt, residents vigorously opposed a 1987 proposal to build houses on what is today the Greenbelt North Woods. Today, the forest's 200 acres are owned either by the City of Greenbelt or by Greenbelt Homes, Inc., the town's housing cooperative. The forest is part of the Greenbelt National Historical Landmark.

Now, the Greenbelt North Woods is caught in a tug of war. Natural processes work to keep the forest healthy and enable the century-old forest to continue maturing. Working against them are the pressures inherent to an inner suburb of Washington DC such as pollution, plants escaping gardens, a deer population ready to explode, and threats of new transportation projects. For now, the North Woods remains a haven for rare orchids, expanses of delicate clubmoss, and a few old trees whose trunks are more than three feet in diameter. May this book be your passport to this wild place.

Opposite: The dirt road along the southern boundary of the Greenbelt North Woods on March 21, 2018.

1

Trees

The plants described in this chapter typically grow with a single woody trunk, the hallmark of a tree. The next chapter describes bushes, which typically have multiple trunks emanating from a single rootball.

Oaks

Trunk of a mature tree, 1/3 life-size (above). Acorn, enlarged (left). Twig with bud and leaf scar, enlarged (right).

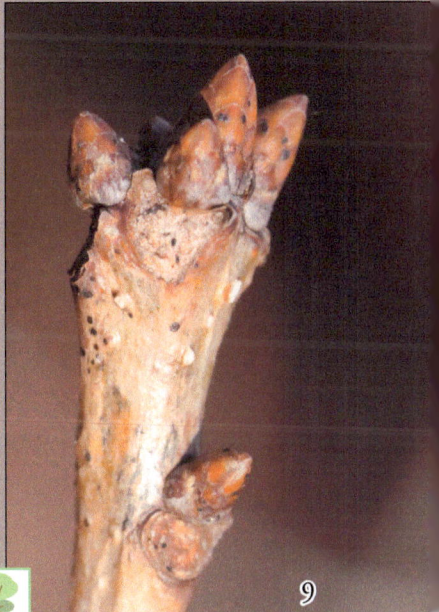

OAKS

scarlet oak

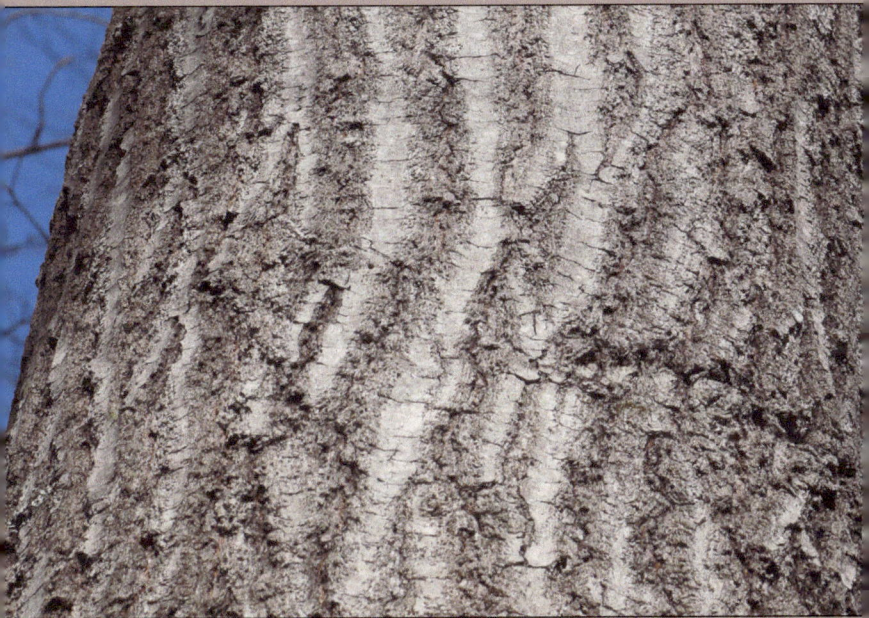

Trunk of a mature tree, 1/3 life-size (above). Acorn, enlarged (left). Twig with bud and leaf scar, enlarged (right).

Oaks

willow oak

Assorted leaves, life-size (opposite). Seedling (above). Acorn, enlarged (left). Trunk of a mature tree (right).

13

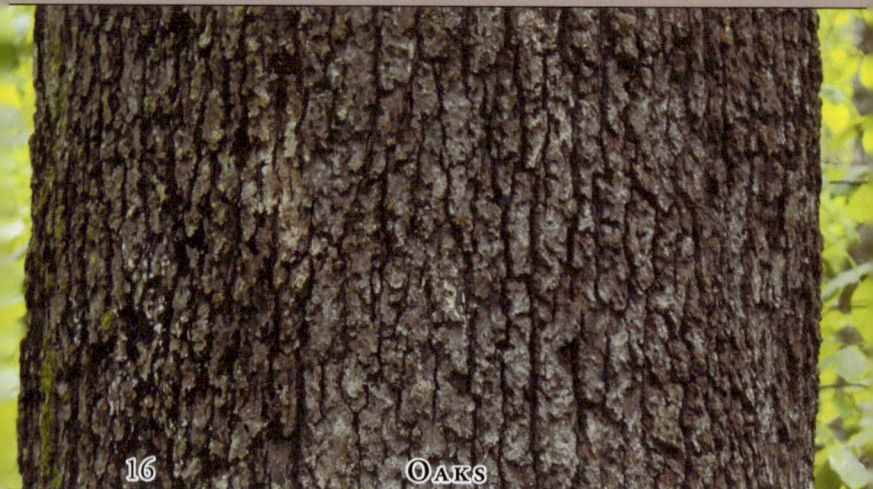

white oak (*Quercus alba*). A white oak leaf has five to ten rounded lobes that extend more than 1/3 of the way to the leaf's central vein. Compared with the browns and grays of many trees' bark, white oak bark appears bleached pale. The bark of a mature white oak may break into narrow, vertical strips along the trunk. These strips are detached on one side and several feet long. White oak acorns have caps that are covered in bumps rather than scales.

LORE: White oak has been Maryland's state tree since 1941 (MD State Archives 2019). The most famous white oak in Maryland was the 460-year-old "Wye Oak" that grew in Wye, Maryland. The tree was destroyed by a thunderstorm in 2002 (Wikipedia, Wye Oak). The heartwood of white oak has clogged pores, which allows it to resist rot better than other oak species. For this reason, white oak has been used in shipbuilding since colonial times (Peattie 1948).

HISTORY: In the late 1700s and early 1800s, the land parcels were first surveyed in and around the Greenbelt North Woods. In those surveys, white oak was by far the most common "first corner" tree (Alan Virta 2017, private communication).

As of 2017, the Greenbelt North Woods has five white oaks with diameters greater than 36 inches: two southeast of Blueberry Hill along Goddard Branch, two southeast of 8G Plateau Place, and one southeast of 8L Laurel Hill Road along a tributary to Canyon Creek (See map on pg. 241). The age of these giant white oaks is uncertain because trunk diameter is only loosely correlated with age. In the forests of Maryland's coastal plain, trees typically take 2 to 20 years to add an inch to their trunk diameter at chest height. The growth rate varies with factors such as soil, amount of sun, crowding, tree age, and tree species. The table below lists the largest oak trees near or in the Greenbelt North Woods for which the author been able to count annual growth rings.

Annual Growth Rings of Selected Oak Trees

Rings [a]	Diameter [a]	Height [a]	When found
White Oak			
130	32 in.	16 in.	May 2019 [b]
140	34.5 in.	24 in.	Aug. 2017 [c]
156	41 in.	16 in.	Nov. 2019 [d]
Red Oak Group			
133	29.6 in.	10 ft.	March 2018 [e]
145	30-39 in.	12 in.	Nov. 2017 [f]

(a) "Rings" is the number of annual growth rings, "Diameter" is the trunk's diameter at the height that the rings were counted, and "Height" is the height at which the rings were counted. (b) A stump between the Greenbelt museum at 10 Crescent Rd. and the nearby playground. (c) A stump on the northeast shore of Greenbelt Lake (*News Review*, 17 Aug 2017). (d) A stump between the southeast shore of the Greenbelt Lake fore-pond and 38 Lakeside Dr. (e) An increment-borer core taken from a fallen tree, 100 feet south of Northway Rd. at the GHI/City-of-Greenbelt property line. (f) A stump 100 feet south of 8G Plateau Pl. Because this stump was cut so close to the ground, the root flare made it difficult to estimate the diameter.

scarlet oak (*Quercus coccinea*). The leaf has about ten, pointed lobes that often extend 3/4 or more of the way to the leaf's central vein. Scarlet oak and white oak are the most common oak species in the Greenbelt North Woods.

SIMILAR SPECIES: Unlike black oak (pg. 20) and northern red oak (*Q. rubra*), the leaves of scarlet oak outline negative space between the lobes that curves back on itself like the liberty bell or a horseshoe. This shape is depicted on the left side of the adjacent illustration. This shape contrasts with the negative space between the lobes of other oak-species leaves, which is typically U-shaped or V-shaped. Avoid the mistake of confusing scarlet oak with northern red oak by remembering that the lobes of a northern red oak leaf are shallow, usually extending no more than half way to the central leaf vein. Northern red oak is common in the Eastern US, but people familiar with the Greenbelt North Woods believe that northern red oak is rare in or absent here.

LORE: Scarlet oak bark is thinner than that of most oaks, so it is more easily damaged by fire (Stein et al. 2003). The leaves in autumn can turn a particularly saturated shade of cranberry red. Once the trunk grows a foot or two in diameter, the bark has flat vertical meandering strips that resemble downhill-skiing trails on a mountainside.

Scarlet oak is a member of the "red oak" group. One easy-to-see characteristic shared by species in the red oak group is that they have leaves with a hair-like spur sticking out of the end of each leaf lobe. In the Greenbelt North Woods, the red oak group is represented by scarlet oak, willow oak, southern red oak, black oak, and blackjack oak (*Quercus marilandica*, not pictured in this book). The other major group is called the "white oak" group, and in the Greenbelt North Woods, it is represented by many white oaks, a few chestnut oaks (see next page), and a few post oaks (*Quercus stellata*, not pictured).

HISTORY: The author has counted the growth rings of a few oaks in the red oak group that blew down or were cut down in the Greenbelt North Woods. As stated in the table on the preceding page, two trees in the red oak group had either 133 or 145 annual growth rings (see also pg. 21).

willow oak (*Quercus phellos*). The finger-like leaf can be anywhere from 2 to 10 inches long. Willow oak has the smallest acorns of any oak species in the Greenbelt North Woods. They are typically less than 1/2 inch long. Willow oak is common along the Mid-Atlantic Coastal Plain and the Southeast US. It prefers moist soil.

chestnut oak (*Quercus montana* preferred over *Quercus prinus*). The leaf has many shallow waves along its edge. Leaf shape is the only way in which the chestnut oak resembles American chestnut (*Castanea dentata*), a tree species that was essentially wiped out in the early 1900s by the chestnut-blight fungus. The bark of chestnut oak is particularly thick and forms deep, vertical ridges that terminate abruptly. LORE: Beech (pg. 58) and chinquapin (pg. 59) have similarly shaped leaves: oval with wavy edges.

southern red oak (*Quercus falcata*). The tree has a wide variety of leave shapes, most of them not symmetric about the leaf's central vein. Southern red oak is the oak species in the Greenbelt North Woods with the most asymmetric and variable leaf shape.

black oak (*Quercus velutina*). Black oak has by far the largest leaves of any oak species in the Greenbelt North Woods (8–12 inches long). Black oak's bark is darker than that of most other oak species. A black oak acorn can be identified by the scales that cover its cap. These scales stick up slightly from the cap, while the scales of other oak species are flat against the cap (http://www.efloras.org, *Quercus velutina*).

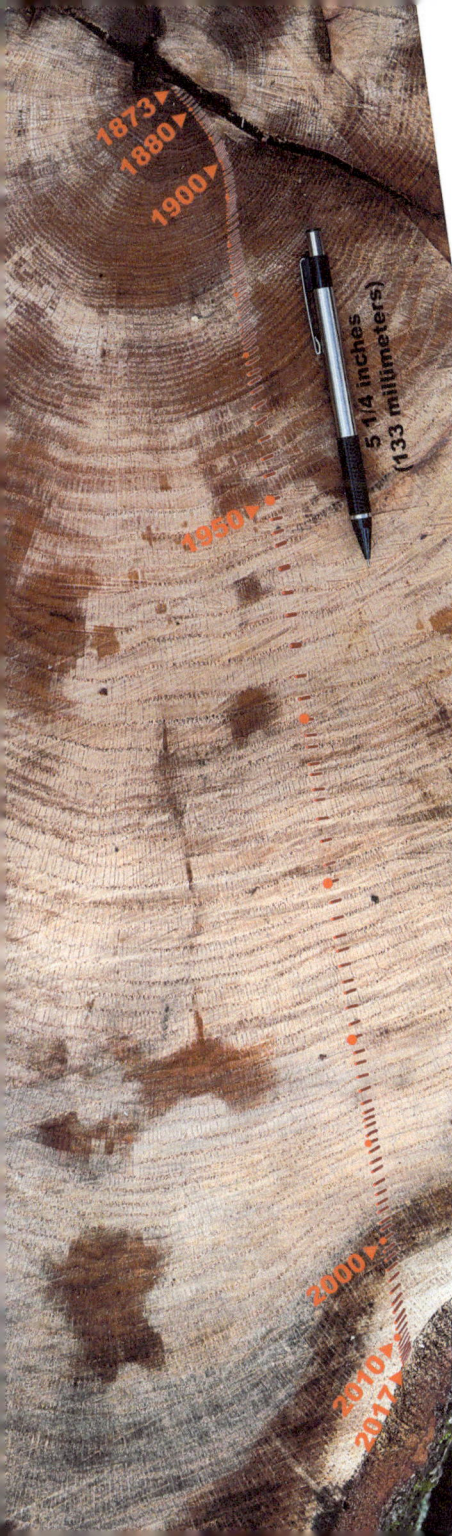

The stump that the author discovered in November 2017, recently cut, in the Greenbelt North Woods. The tree was located about 100 feet from the forest edge, east of 8G Plateau Place. From the appearance of the bark and wood, the tree was likely a member of the red oak group. As shown in this photo, the stump had 145 annual growth rings. The number of growth rings suggests that the acorn that produced this tree had sprouted and reached a 1-foot height in 1873. In the vicinity of this tree, there was likely a forest canopy in the year 1873 because oak seedlings have trouble surviving in a meadow or crop field. In 1941, this tree began a growth spurt, which was the same year that the federal government built the townhomes nearby on Plateau Place. Growth slowed around 2008. It is unclear why the tree was cut down in 2017. The stump was cut about 1 foot aboveground. The tree was located on land owned by Greenbelt Homes, Inc. The author attempted to avoid the roof flair when he estimated a stump diameter of 30.3–39.4 inches.

21

tulip poplar

Trunk (above). Seed cone and samara (left). Twig with bud (below). Flower bud (bottom).

Flower (above). Leaf from a sapling (below).

tulip poplar

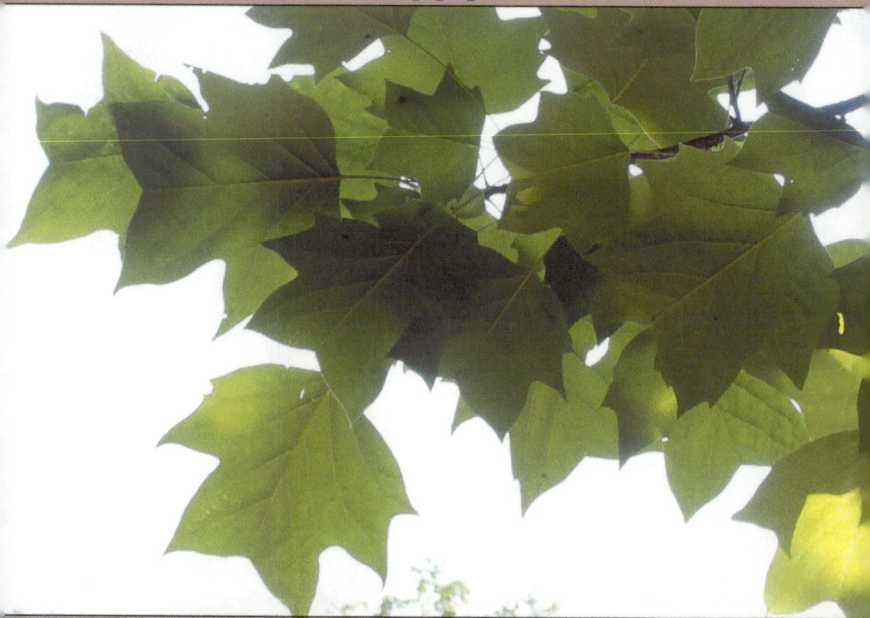

Leaves (above). Four-inch-diameter trunk (left). Buds and
central axis of a seed cone (right).

tulip poplar

Leaves (above). Four-inch-diameter trunk (left). Buds and central axis of a seed cone (right).

LOBED LEAVES

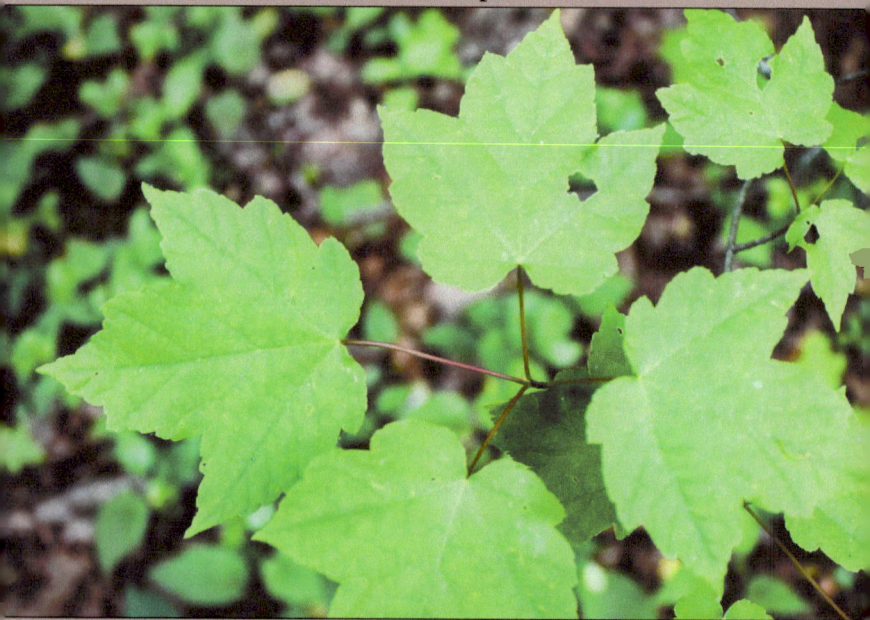

Leaves (above). Buds, enlarged (left). Twig and bud, life-size (right).

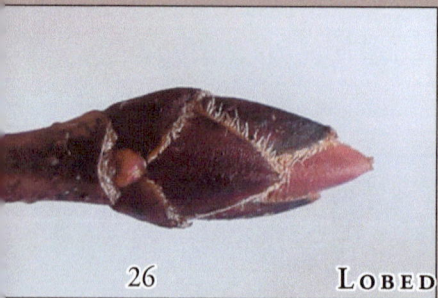

Flowers, 10× life-size (above). Trunk bark showing cracks, 1/4 life-size (left). Samara, 1.5× life-size (right).

Seed ball, 3× life-size (above). Trunk of a mature tree (left). Twig with a leaf scar and bud (right).

Leaf in autumn (above). Twig with cork growths (left). Sapling trunk with cork growths (below). Flower (bottom).

sycamore

Bark on a mature trunk (above). Seed ball (left). End of a leaf
stem (right).

sycamore

Leaf (above). Twig and bud (left). Bud, enlarged (right).

tulip poplar; yellow poplar; tulip-tree
(*Liriodendron tulipifera*). The only tree species in the
Greenbelt North Woods whose typical leaf has four
lobes, two on either side of the leaf's central vein. The
flower is spherical, 2 inches in diameter. The flower
petals are green-white with orange highlights. The
flower's matchstick-shaped stamens are pale yellow
or cream colored. The tree prefers moist soil but will
grow under a wide variety of conditions. Tulip poplar
grows faster than oak in height and trunk diameter. It's
branches are likely to blow down in windstorms, and the
shallow roots make the entire tree susceptible to being
blown over. In winter, the bud is flat like a duck's bill.
The leaves turn bright yellow in autumn.

HISTORY: In the Greenbelt North Woods, the trees
with the largest-diameter trunks are tulip poplar. There
are several tulip poplars with a trunk diameter at chest
height of at least 3½ feet. Five such trees grow along
Goddard Branch, one is in a cove on the east side of
Blueberry Hill and the other four are within 200 feet of
the Greenbelt Homes Inc. (GHI) homes along the east
side of Laurel Hill Road. These large tulip poplars are
not necessarily older than the nearby oaks because tulip
poplar grows so quickly.

LORE: Tulip poplar is the state tree of Indiana,
Kentucky, and Tennessee (Choukas-Bradley 2004). Tulip
poplar lumber is often referred to "poplar" in hardware
stores, but tulip poplar is not a true poplar. Instead,
tulip poplar is more closely related to magnolia trees
(both are in the family Magnoliaceae). You might guess
this relationship because tulip poplar's flower somewhat
resembles a magnolia flower.

sassafras (*Sassafras albidum*). Sassafras is the only tree species in the Greenbelt North Woods with precisely three leaf shapes: mitten, oval, and what might be called "double-thumb mitten." It is a pioneer species.

red maple (*Acer rubrum*). A red maple leaf has three pointy lobes and is rather small (3 inches long). The bark is smooth in saplings, cracked in larger trees. In March, clusters of small red flowers bloom before the leaves come out. Winged seeds resemble helicopters as they fall to the ground in late spring. Red maple prefers moist soil.

SIMILAR SPECIES: Only a few tree species in the Greenbelt North Woods have twigs that grow in pairs, on opposite sides of the branch, 🌱. Among the canopy trees (trees growing 50–120 feet tall), red maple is the only species with opposite twigs. Opposite twigs are more common among understory trees, bushes, and vines such as dogwood (pg. 63), amur honeysuckle (pg. 88), and plants in the genus *Euonymus* (pg. 100).

LORE: Red maple will grow in such moist soil that many of the oldest red maples in the Greenbelt North Woods have heart rot. Heart rot describes a trunk hollowed out by fungal rot. A number of the large red maples in the Goddard Branch floodplain (>24 inch diameter at chest height) have had their trunks snapped in two by storms in 2017 and 2018, revealing hollow trunks. Solid wood was only a few inches thick under the bark. During the past century, red maple has become one of the most numerous tree species in the Eastern US, perhaps because of government efforts to prevent wildfire. Previously, forest fire had reduced the red maple population because the tree's thin bark is easily damaged by fire (Abrams 1998, 2000, 2003).

sweetgum (*Liquidambar styraciflua*). The leaf has five long lobes that each end in a point. The leaf's edge has inconspicuous teeth. A sapling may have corky bumps on its trunk or 1/2-inch-tall corky ridges running for several inches along the length of a twig. The seed ball, commonly called a "gum ball," is about 1½ inches across and is covered with dozens of "beaks." The tree prefers moist soil. SIMILAR SPECIES: Both sweetgum and sycamore have five-pointed leaves, but the five points of sweetgum are much longer and the bark of the two trees are very different. The corky ridges on some sweetgum twigs resemble those on the twigs of common hackberry (*Celtis occidentalis*). The two tree species have very different leaf shape: common hackberry has a spade-shaped leaf with a heart-shaped base and pointed tip, ♠.

sycamore (*Platanus occidentalis*). The leaf has three or sometimes five lobes that each end in a pointed tip. The lobe's pointed tip is hook-like and matches the hook-like teeth along the rest of the leaf edge. On the trunk of a mature tree, the smooth bark comes off in patches with varying shades of gray. The bark pattern resembles the gray camouflage pattern of some military uniforms. The seed ball is 1½ inches in diameter. It is hard and knobby when immature and becomes a fluffy puffball when the seeds have finished maturing. Sycamore prefers full sun, so it typically grows at the forest's edge. This photo of the bark is from a mature tree outside of the Greenbelt North Woods (in front of the Greenbelt Library). There are only a handful of sycamores along the edge or deep within the Greenbelt North Woods.

black locust

Trunk of a mature tree (above). Flower (left). Leaves far above (right). Thorns on a sampling's branch (bottom right).

35

COMPOUND LEAVES

mockernut hickory

Leaflet (top left). Bark of a mature tree (top right). Leaf scar on
a branch (bottom left). Bud, enlarged (bottom right).

pignut hickory

Leaf (above). Leaf emerging from bud (below). Trunk of a mature tree (left). Trunk of a sapling (right).

39

black walnut

Leaves overhead (above). Trunk (left). Leaflet (right).

COMPOUND LEAVES

tree of heaven

Leaflets & a cluster of samara (top left). Leaves (right). Leaf scar on a branch (bottom left). Glands at the base of a leaf (right).

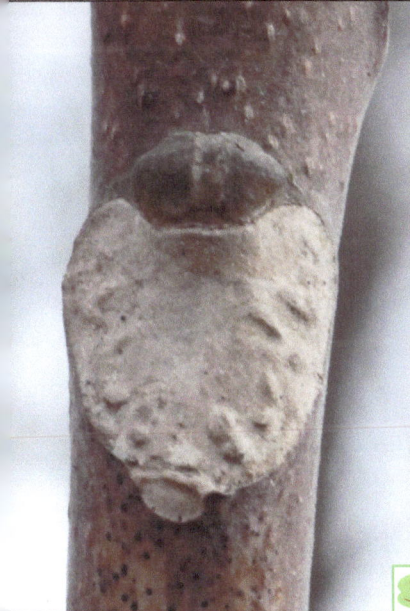

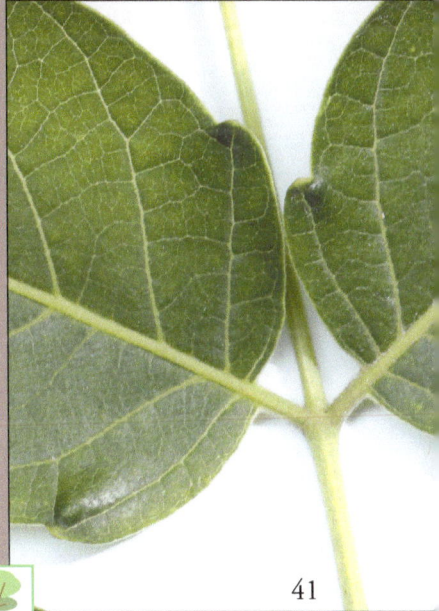

The leaf of a woody plant is a food-producing organ that grows from a single bud regardless of whether the leaf is simple or compound. A compound leaf has multiple leaf blades on a single leaf stem, all growing from a single bud. An individual blade is called a "leaflet," and in most species, leaflets are arranged along a length of the leaf stem. In a few species, the leaflets all join the leaf stem at a single point.

black locust (*Robinia pseudoacacia*). The compound leaf has 12–18 pairs of oval leaflets. The branches of saplings may be armed with pairs of 3/4-inch-long spikes, one pair near each leaf scar. Like the redbud tree, black locust is a member of the pea family and has pea-like seed pods. SIMILAR SPECIES: While not found in the Greenbelt North Woods, honey locust (*Gleditsia triacanthos*) has branched thorns several inches long, unlike black locust's unbranched thorns. Sumac (*Rhus*) trees have compound leaves similar in shape to black locust's, but no thorns and a very different flower shape. LORE: At present, the official habitat of black locust is narrow: Arkansas and the southern Appalachian Mountains. Black locust is known as a pioneer species because it is one of the first trees to grow when the forest reclaims an abandoned field. Black locust wood resists rot and was logged commercially until approximately 1900 when the locust borer beetle (*Megacyllene robiniae*) decimated the population.

mockernut hickory (*Carya tomentosa* also known as *Carya alba*). The compound leaf has seven to nine leaflets each 4–8 inches long. The nut has four sides and is roughly spherical. When it falls from the tree,

▲ Outline of pawpaw leaf, life-size.

the nut is contained in a husk that is about 1/4 inch thick and 1½ inches in diameter. SIMILAR SPECIES: If the nut husk is thin, like paper, then the species may be bitternut hickory (*C. cordiformis*), not mockernut. Both bitternut and mockernut have seven to nine leaflets. In the Greenbelt North Woods, a hickory tree with only five leaflets is likely to be pignut (see next entry). LORE: One might describe part of the Greenbelt North Woods as an oak-hickory forest, a common forest type in Maryland. Compared with the oak trees, the hickories in the Greenbelt North Woods tend to have smaller-diameter trunks, which to a first approximation suggests that the hickory population is younger than the oak population. In the North Woods, the author has found dozens of oaks trees with trunks over 30 inches in diameter, but only one hickory tree with a trunk this stout.

pignut hickory (*Carya glabra*). The compound leaf has five leaflets each 3–6 inches long. The nut is contained within an elongated or fig-shaped husk about 1¼ inches long. The nut falls in August when the husk is still green, although the husk turns brown-black after sitting on the ground for a while.

SIMILAR SPECIES: It can be difficult to distinguish a hickory leaflet from a black gum leaf (pg. 62) or pawpaw leaf (*Asimina triloba*). The pawpaw tree is not pictured in this field guide because it isn't found in the Greenbelt North Woods. A few pawpaw grow nearby in the Hamilton Woods. A life-size outline of a pawpaw leaf is shown on this page in gray. A pawpaw leaf is large (10–12 inches long), which is the easiest way to distinguish it from hickory or black gum. Pawpaw is native to North America and was once commercially grown in the US. Pawpaw fruit is said to taste like a tropical fruit. Many people today are unaware of this tree species (Moore, 2017).

box elder (*Acer negundo*). The compound leaf has three to five leaflets, each with one or two thumbs. The species prefers full sun. The few box elders that grow at the forest edge along Northway Road are young and under 20 feet tall. A few box elders are also found in the interior of the Greenbelt North Woods. SIMILAR SPECIES: Box elder's leaves can be startlingly similar in appearance to those of poison ivy (pg. 113).

mimosa tree; pink silk tree (*Albizia julibrissin*). The compound leaf resembles a fern frond. In summer, the tree's flowers are shaped like pink fluff-balls. In autumn, the tree has pea-like seed pods, which makes sense because it is in the pea family (Fabaceae). LORE: The mimosa tree was imported to the US from Asia in the 1700s. It is a pioneer species, like black locust and tree of heaven, two species described elsewhere in this section. The Latin name *julibrissin* comes from the Persian word for "silk flower" (Wikipedia, *Albizia julibrissin*).

black walnut (*Juglans nigra*). The compound leaf has 6–12 pairs of leaflets. Each pair of leaflets has one leaflet on either side of the leaf stem, and there is no final, unpaired leaflet at the end of the leaf stem. Each leaflet is oval with a pointed tip and fine, serrated teeth. Black walnut is rare in the Greenbelt North Woods, but a large one can be found near the source of Canyon Creek. Black walnut is grown as a landscaping tree, such as at the intersection of Hillside and Laurel Hill Roads.

The nut's hard shell is covered by a husk that is firm, fleshy, and nearly spherical. The outside of the husk is pale green with a rough texture in summer, turning black when ripe. The husk is roughly 2 inches in diameter, and it smells like spiced apple cider. The husk's black flesh can stain clothing and skin. Walnuts still in their shell can be found in the grocery store, but naked,

The husks of a black walnut (left) and hickory (right), still green shortly after falling from the tree, life-size.

unopened shells are hard to find in the forest. This is because the husk still covers the shell when the nut falls from the tree, and by the time the husk decomposes, animals have often gnawed off part of the shell to reach the nut meat.

SIMILAR SPECIES: Distinguish black walnut from tree of heaven by black walnut's leaf stems being green (not red) and black walnut's leaves being less long and lacking the leaf-base gland of tree of heaven. The husks of hickory and walnut are a similar color, but hickory husks are smaller and smoother. In the picture above, compare the husks of a freshly fallen black walnut (left) and hickory (right). Unlike all other compound-leaf trees in the Greenbelt North Woods, black walnut has an even number of leaflets, i.e., black walnut does *not* have an unpaired leaflet sticking out of the end of the leaf stem (Choukas-Bradley 2008, pg. 156).

Poison sumac (*Toxicodendron vernix*) has a compound leaf similar to that of black walnut, except that poison sumac has a single leaflet sticking out of the end of the compound leaf. Touching a poison sumac leaf can cause a rash. Nonetheless, ecologists are protective of poison sumac because it is either uncommon or absent throughout much of its native range in the Eastern US. Currently, only one poison sumac tree is known to be growing in the Greenbelt North Woods, and it is located in a small cove on the southeast side of Blueberry Hill.

LORE: Black walnut is a pioneer species, meaning that it can help the forest reclaim an abandoned field but also that its seedlings need full-sun to grow. Black walnut seedlings are unlikely to grow in the deep shade of an established forest. Black walnut is grown commercially for both the tree's edible nuts and for its timber (Hilgedick 2017). In the US, the vast majority of walnut trees grown for their nuts are English walnut (*Juglans regia*), not black walnut.

tree of heaven (*Ailanthus altissima*). The compound leaf has 5–12 pairs of leaflets. Each leaflet is long and triangular in shape and has a gland on one side or both sides of the leaflet's base. At this time, only a few specimens are found in the Greenbelt North Woods, all at the edge of the forest. LORE: Tree of heaven is a bizarrely hearty, invasive tree that is able to tolerate pollution and drought. It was introduced to the US from China in the 1700s. It re-sprouts vigorously from its roots if cut down. It is one of the fastest growing trees in North America, able to add 3–6 feet to its height in a year.

Leaf in autumn, life-size (above). Bud (below), nut and bur (bottom left), all 2× life-size. Trunk, 1/5 life-size (right).

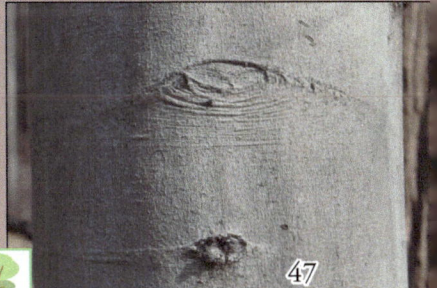

OVAL LEAVES

elm

Leaves (above). Trunk of a mature tree (below).

49

Leaves (above). Trunk (below).

OVAL LEAVES

ironwood

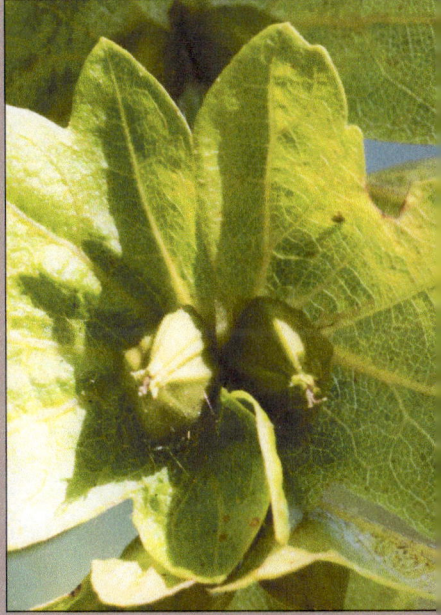

Double-toothed leaf edge (above left). Seed pods, 2× life-size
(above right). Twig (below left). Bud, enlarged (below right).

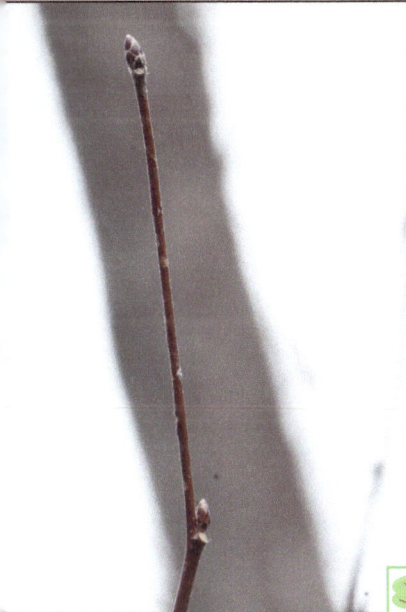

Trunk of a mature tree (above). Leaf (below). Glands at base of a leaf, 5× life-size (bottom left). Flower (bottom right).

callery pear

Leaves and unripe fruit (above). Bark of a mature tree (left). Flower (right).

actual
size

Flower, 4× life-size (above). Bud, 3× life-size (left). Leaves (right).

actual size

beech (*Fagus grandifolia*). Beech leaves are oval with coarse teeth and straight side veins that are oriented parallel to each other, 🍃. The trunk's bark is pale and smooth. Parchment-colored dead leaves can remain on a sapling through winter and spring until the new year's leaves come out.

SIMILAR SPECIES: Considered together, a beech tree's leaf shape and smooth bark distinguishes it from other tree species. Beech's leaf shape (but not bark) resembles that ironwood (pg. 59) and the far-less-common chinquapin (pg. 59). Beech's bark (but not leaf shape) resembles that of holly and red maple (pg. 62, 33).

LORE: Beech trees are very tolerant of shade, and they themselves produce deep shade. Beech seedlings can grow in such deep shade, but not oak or tulip poplar seedlings. The thin bark of a beech tree helps it to outcompete other species in deep shade. Sunlight penetrates the thin bark to reach the layer just underneath that contains chlorophyll. This layer can produce food to supplement the food produced by the tree's leaves. The disadvantage of thin bark is that a brush fire can easily kill the tree.

ECOLOGICAL MYSTERY: There are no large beech trees in the Greenbelt North Woods (trunks over 20 inches in diameter), and no beech grove either. The reason is unknown. In contrast, stout beech trees and beech groves do exist in nearby forests such as the city-owned forest around Greenbelt Lake, the city-owned Indian Creek Park, Greenbelt Park (owned by the National Park Service), and the state-owned conservation land south of the Greenbelt Metro Station.

chinquapin (*Castanea pumila*). The leaf is oval with coarse teeth and straight, parallel side veins, . The nut ripens in autumn and is covered in a 1-inch-diameter spiny burr. The tree prefers dry sandy soil. A few chinquapin saplings are found on the north side of Blueberry Hill. **LORE:** Chinquapin is a dwarf species in the chestnut genus. Chinquapin is somewhat resistant to the chestnut blight fungus that essentially eradicated American chestnut (*C. dentata*) in the early 1900s. Prior to the construction of Greenbelt, chinquapin trees were more plentiful in this area and residents would harvest nuts from trees growing in the wild (Jim Soule, private communication, 2017).

elm; American elm (*Ulmus americanus*). The oval leaf is double toothed with a pointed tip and straight, parallel side veins, . Double toothed means that small teeth are superimposed on large teeth, . The seed forms inside of a 1-inch-diameter flat disk. This seed-bearing structure is called a samara. A samara is a dry fruit that consists of both a papery-thin wing-like structure and a seed. The wing causes the fruit to spin as it falls, the spinning slows the fruit's fall, and that delay gives the wind more time to spread the fruit far from the parent tree. **SIMILAR SPECIES:** Elm leaves have an uneven base, , unlike the leaves of beech, ironwood, and chinquapin. Both elm and ironwood have double-toothed leaves, but their bark is different. **LORE:** Almost a hundred years ago, Dutch elm disease (a fungus spread by bark beetles) killed the elm trees that lined many city streets. Elms still grow wild in forests in Maryland and elsewhere. Use the name "American elm" when necessary to distinguish this species from "slippery elm" (*U. rubra*).

ironwood; musclewood; American hornbeam (*Carpinus caroliniana*). The leaf is oval and double toothed, /\/\/\. The leaf has straight, parallel veins, , and a pointed tip. When the trunk reaches about 3 inches in diameter, it begins to have bulges that are said to resemble bulging muscles, hence an alternative name for ironwood: musclewood. **SIMILAR SPECIES:** Ironwood leaves are similar to elm except that ironwood leaves have a symmetric base. **LORE:** It is said that farmers used to make tool handles from the extremely hard wood of this species, perhaps leading to the common name "ironwood." Ironwood trees inhabit the forest understory and do not grow large enough for commercial harvesting to be viable.

black cherry (*Prunus serotina*). The oval leaf has fine teeth and a pointed tip, as do the leaves of other cherry species. The bark is smooth on saplings and broken on mature trees (like the bark of pear trees). Black cherry and other species in the *Padus* subgenus of cherry have flowers that are organized into narrow columns that are about 6 inches long. The flower columns are about three times longer than they are wide. Black cherry tends to bloom in late April or early May after the leaves come out. The spherical dark-red cherry fruit is ripe by late summer. Black Cherry is somewhat rare in the Greenbelt North Woods. **LORE:** Black cherry is a member of the rose family, as are pear, apple, blackberry, raspberry, and not surprisingly, multiflora rose. One can see the family resemblance in that these species have individual flowers that are about an inch across with five white, flat petals. Black cherry is a pioneer tree species, growing quickly in breaks in the forest canopy.

cherry in the *Cerasus* subgenus (*Prunus* subgenus *Cerasus*). The oval leaf has fine teeth and a pointed tip, which is a typical shape for most cherry species that grow in the Eastern US. Characteristics that are specific to the *Cerasus* subgenus include smooth slivery-gray slightly shiny bark with very prominent lip-shaped black pores called lenticels on any trunk that is at least 6 inches in diameter. *Cerasus* subgenus cherries are also characterized by flowers that grow individually or in hemispherical, loose bunches. The inch-across flowers have five white or pinkish petals. In Greenbelt, these cherry trees bloom in early April before the leaves come out. Examples include *Prunus avium* (known as sweet cherry or wild cherry) and *Prunus cerasus* (sour cherry). Unlike black cherry, *Cerasus* subgenus cherry is native to Europe and Asia, but not the Eastern US.

SIMILAR SPECIES: The smooth gray bark of *Cerasus* subgenus cherry is somewhat like that of beech, holly, ironwood and (young) red maple. The bark of these cherry trees, however, has its own special color of slivery gray and prominent lenticels resemble an eye or lips, 1/4–1/2 inch across horizontally. While many tree species have small, visible lenticels, the lenticels of *Cerasus* subgenus cherry are large and they stick out from the bark.

The hemispherical flower bunches of *Cerasus* subgenus cherry are similar to those of callery pear (see next entry) and they are unlike the long, dense, cylindrical flower bunches of black cherry (see previous entry).

LORE: Some leaves have a few red dots along the leaf's edge near its base. These dots are glands called extrafloral nectaries. If pests start to eat the leaves, the tree will emit scent from these leaf glands to attract beneficial insects that will eat the pest (Pulice and Packer 2008).

callery pear (*Pyrus calleryana*). The oval leaf is somewhat egg shaped with fine teeth, a pointed tip, and a flat base, . In April, the flower blooms before the leaves come out. The flowers are about 1 inch across, are composed of five bright-white petals, and are arranged in hemispherical bunches with about ten flowers to a bunch. Callery pear grows along Northway Road and the edge of the Northway athletic fields, and saplings can be found deeper in the forest. The fruit is a green-brown sphere 1/2 inch in diameter. The fruit may be present on branches from July through winter.

LORE: Callery pear is an invasive species that includes a variety known as "bradford pear." A botanist would say that bradford pear is a cultivar of callery pear. In the early 1900s, a bacterial disease called "fire blight" decimated many commercial pear orchards, and in response, callery pear was imported from East Asia as rootstock. In the 1960s, the bradford cultivar was developed and widely planted as a landscaping tree.

holly (*Ilex opaca*). Thick, leathery, dark-green leaves have sharp points along their edge. Each leaf lasts about 3 years, giving the tree an evergreen appearance. Bright-red spherical berries are 1/4 inch in diameter. The berries ripen in autumn and may remain on the tree in winter. Holly trees form thickets that shade the forest floor so densely that undergrowth may be absent. Holly avoids swampy soil. LORE: Holly leaves and berries are traditionally used to construct Christmas wreaths. It is unlawful to harvest holly, or other plants, from the Greenbelt Forest Preserve.

black gum; tupelo (*Nyssa sylvatica*). The approximately oval leaf has a smooth edge. Some leaves have their widest part near the leaf tip . Looking up into a mature black gum tree, one may find that its trunk is less than perfectly straight and its branches crooked, giving the tree a disheveled appearance. LORE: Black gum grow in a wide range of climate and soil. The species is shade tolerant, fire tolerant, and capable of living for centuries (Abrams 2007). Its fall foliage can be saturated yellow, orange, red, or purple. Another name for black gum is "tupelo," which is a Native American word for "swamp tree" (Wikipedia, *Nyssa sylvatica*).

dogwood; flowering dogwood (*Cornus florida*). Dogwood trees are generally under 20 feet tall and blend into their surrounding except when they bloom. In April, the large four-petaled flat, white flower (several inches wide) reveals the locations of the few dogwood trees scattered through the Greenbelt North Woods. Terminal buds that will become flowers are shaped like miniature garlic bulbs in winter (1/4 to 1/2 inch across). The last 6 inches of many twigs turn upward, a characteristic that no other tree species in this forest shares. Buds that will open into leaves are shaped like ice-cream cones. The leaf is oval with a pointed tip, smooth edge, and veins that curve toward the tip of the leaf, 🍃. The leaves are arranged in pairs on opposites sides of the branch, ⚘. In September, the clusters of half-a-dozen ellipsoidal berries turn bright red. In October, dogwood leaves turn a deep, saturated red-purple. Other trees in the North Woods that may display an equally saturated red-purple are sweetgum and black gum (pg. 34, 62).

LORE: Dogwood is the state tree and flower of Virginia. In the late 1900s, a fungus almost wiped out dogwoods from the Eastern US. The disease that the dogwoods suffered from is called "dogwood anthracnose" and the cause of the disease is the fungus *Discula destructiva* (Choukas-Bradley 2008, pg. 349; Higgins 2017). The remaining dogwoods are still susceptible to this disease.

redbud

Leaves (above). Trunk (below).

SPADE-SHAPED LEAVES

Flowers (above). Seed pods (below).

SPADE-SHAPED LEAVES

Leaves (above). Trunk (below).

redbud (*Cercis canadensis*). The leaf is spade-shaped, and it is 4–6 inches long with a smooth edge and a pointed tip. The leaf stem has a collar where the leaf veins meet at the base of the leaf. In spring, clusters of pink flowers grow on the trunk or branches. In autumn, the seed pod resembles a pea pod, 3–5 inches long, growing in clusters. The bark is striped.

SIMILAR SPECIES: Redbud's leaf shape is similar to that of two other tree species that are occasionally found in Greenbelt outside of the North Woods: princess paulownia (*Paulownia tomentosa*) and northern catalpa (*Catalpa speciosa*). The non-native princess paulownia has fig-shaped seed pods (1½ inches long) and leaves of variable shape: heart shaped or five lobed. Northern catalpa has pea-like seed pods that are 10 inches long or longer. Northern catalpa's leaf and seed pod are both twice as long as those of redbud. Northern catalpa is native to the western US and Canada, but not Maryland.

HABITAT: Redbud prefers the forest edge. The author has found redbud along Northway Road and the edge of the Northway athletic fields. The species is rare in the Greenbelt North Woods.

LORE: Redbud is the state tree of Oklahoma. As redbud is a member of the pea family, the shape of its flowers and seed pods resemble those of green beans and pea plants grown in home gardens. Like other members of the pea family, redbud can fix nitrogen from the air with the help of soil bacteria (MacKay 2013, pg. 91). Authorities disagree about whether redbud is native throughout Maryland, but it is undisputedly native to parts of the Eastern US (Sullivan 1994 vs. Kartesz 2015).

eastern cottonwood (*Populus deltoides*). The approximately triangular leaf has a wavy edge and a pointed tip. A breeze is sufficient to set the leaves trembling. The smooth bark develops vertical cracks as the trunk grows wider than about 6 inches in diameter. The species is rare in the Greenbelt North Woods. A few trees are found at the forest edge along Northway Road. SIMILAR SPECIES: Eastern cottonwood leaves are similar to those of big-toothed aspen (*Populus grandidentata*) and quaking aspen (*P. tremuloides*). Eastern cottonwood leaves can be distinguished by their more numerous teeth and their flat base.

3x life-size

2/3×
life-
size

PINES

loblolly pine

Trunk (above). Pine cone (below).

71

actual
size

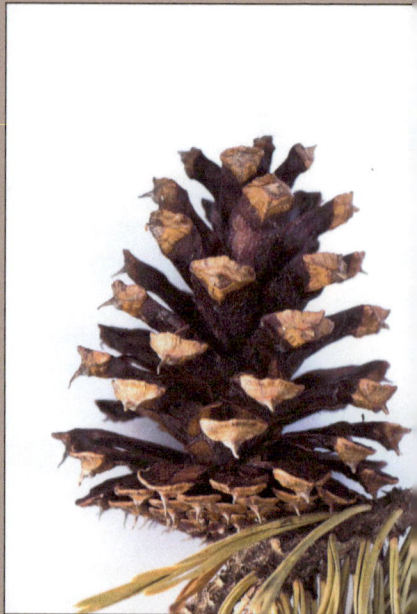

Needles (above left). Pine cone (right). Trunk (below).

1 inch

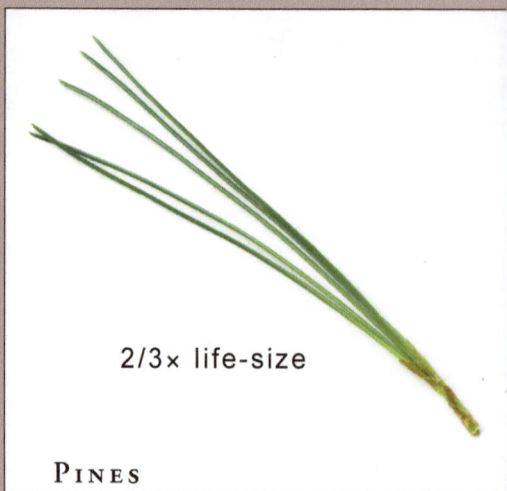

2/3× life-size

PINES

In Maryland's coastal plain, pine trees tend to be
pioneer species. As best we can tell, many farm fields
were abandoned in the late 1800s in the Greenbelt area.
Thereafter, pine trees were the most successful trees to
compete with meadow plants in many areas of Prince
George's County (Besley 1913, pg. 6–7). Once the pines
formed a canopy, their shade suppressed the meadow
plants, which gave oak, maple, and other deciduous
trees a chance to grow. Eventually, these deciduous trees
produced even denser shade, which then prevented pine
seedlings from growing. Today, the North Woods has no
pine seedlings, but a number of large pine trees that are
relics of the earlier pine-dominated era, the late 1800s
and early 1900s.

Virginia pine (*Pinus virginiana*). The short needles
(2 inches long) come in bunches of two. For a pine tree,
many things about Virginia pine are small. Compared
with other pine species growing here, Virginia pine
has smaller cones, shorter needles, and smaller bark
"nuggets" on its trunk. Even Virginia pine's native
growth range is small: New Jersey to Virginia and from
the Atlantic coast inland to Tennessee. LORE: Virginia
pine quickly colonizes abandoned fields, but it is a
short-lived pine species. While loblolly pine and pitch
pine can live over 250 years, Virginia pine rarely lives
longer than 65–90 years (Burns 1990). Virginia pine's
short lifespan is related to it blowing down easily due
to shallow roots and to it being prone to heartwood rot
(Wikipedia, Virginia pine; Burns 1990). Consistent with
this information, the author found two Virginia pines
blown down by the March 2, 2018 windstorm. Located
along the southern edge of the North Woods, these two
pine were each 15 inches in diameter at chest height

and had 68 or 71 annual grown rings. Although no pine seedlings exist in the Greenbelt North Woods today, the age of these two trees suggest that forest was still hospitable to pine seedlings a decade after the founding of Greenbelt in 1937.

loblolly pine (*Pinus taeda*). The very long needles (6–11 inches long) come in bunches of three. Loblolly pine grows primarily from New Jersey south along the Atlantic Coast and in the states along the Gulf of Mexico.

pitch pine (*Pinus virginiana*). The 3–4-inch-long needles come in bunches of three. Unlike other pine species, pitch pine may grow tufts of needles on its trunk. The tree has rough, thick bark. Pitch pine is common in coastal New England, Pennsylvania, and in the southern Appalachian Mountains. **Lore:** Pitch pine is better than most tree species at surviving brush fire. Naturalists have found trees in the Greenbelt North Woods that appear to be a hybrid of pitch pine and loblolly pine.

white pine (*Pinus strobus*). The thin, straight needles (3–4 inches long) come in bunches of five. The long, thin pine cone is 4–5 inches long and about 1 inch wide when open. The tree has smooth bark. The branches emanate horizontally from the trunk in whorls. White pine is rare in the Greenbelt North Woods. It prefers climates colder than Greenbelt's, such as the coastal areas from New Jersey north and the entire length of the Appalachian Mountains. In other words, white pine is not native to the part of Maryland that contains Greenbelt, but it is native to other parts of Maryland.

Opposite: The pink capsule of a strawberry bush, *Euonymus americanus* (see pg. 100).

PINES

2

Bushes & Woody Vines

This chapter describes woody plants that lack the single, upright trunk of a tree. Such plants may grow in the form of a bush, a climbing vine, or ground cover. A bush often has several upright stems leaving the ground. Some vines climb by twining around a support while others climb with the assistance of tendrils or aerial roots. Ground-cover plants expand horizontally while staying within a few inches of the ground.

mountain laurel

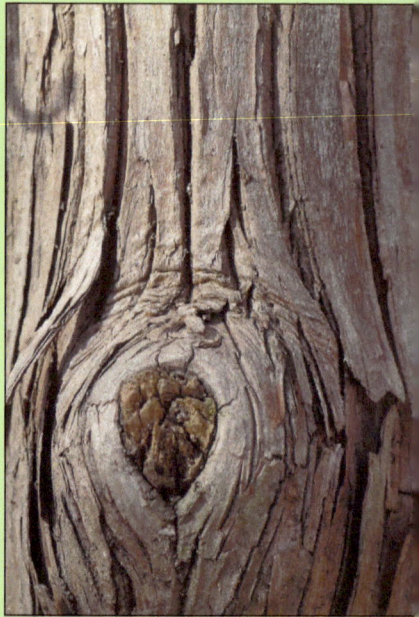

Flower and mature stem, 3× life-size (above). Flower buds (below left). Back of flower (below right).

SMOOTH-EDGED LEAVES

pinkster azalea

Cluster of flowers (above). Seed pod in winter (left). Flower bud, enlarged (right).

blueberry

Leaves and unripe berries (above). Flowers (left). Twig with bud (below).

SMOOTH-EDGED LEAVES

spicebush

actual size

3x life-size

3x life-size   81

partridge berry

4× life-size

2× life-size

periwinkle

amur honeysuckle

Japanese honeysuckle

barberry

Stem with berries in winter, 2× life-size (above). Leaves in summer rain, 3× life-size (below).

SMOOTH-EDGED LEAVES

mountain laurel (*Kalmia latifolia*). The bush has thick dark-green oval leaves and white umbrella-shaped flowers. Like other members of the heath family (see next two entries), mountain laurel has leaves with a smooth edge. In the Greenbelt North Woods, mountain laurel can be found north of Laurel Hill Road, on Blueberry Hill, and on the hill in the forest's northeast corner. Because mountain laurel prefers shade and well-drained soil, it is typically found in the forest interior and on hillsides rather than in floodplains.

SIMILAR SPECIES: Among the heath-family bushes in the Greenbelt North Woods, mountain laurel is the only species with evergreen leaves. Mountain laurel's leaves are also the largest: 3–5 inches long (http://www.efloras.org).

HISTORY: In 2018, the author found one mountain laurel bush in the Greenbelt North Woods that might be over 100 years old. Counting the annual growth rings of dead mountain laurel branches in the Greenbelt North Woods, the author found that these mountain laurels typically took 21 years to add one inch of stem diameter (1.2 millimeters per year). This growth rate can be used to make a rough estimate of the age of the particularly large mountain laurel bush near the BARC fence northeast of Laurel Hill Road. In 2018, this bush had the remarkable diameter of 6 inches at a height of 6 inches aboveground. If the growth rate were 21 years per inch, then this plant would be 126 years old, i.e., it was a six-inch-tall plant in 1892. In 2018, two other mountain laurels nearby were 3.8 inches in diameter 6 inches aboveground, which suggests that they might be 80 years old.

The Maryland Native Plant Society reports that

mountain laurel thickets in several DC area forests have individual plants that are at least 50–60 years old (Choukas-Bradley 2013, pg. 1, 7). The typical lifespan of mountain laurel is said to be 75 years.

LORE: Mountain laurel is the state flower of Pennsylvania. Plants in the heath family typically prefer dry soil, as is found on the top of Blueberry Hill. Some people have described the oak/pine/heath grove at the top of Blueberry Hill as a southern outlier of the pitch pine forests of coastal New Jersey. These New Jersey forests are called "pine barrens."

Some forest-classification systems include a oak/pine/heath association that aptly describes the forest at the top of Blueberry Hill. This portion of the forest contrasts with the oak/tulip-poplar/maple association found a few hundred feet away in the Goddard Branch floodplain. The hilly terrain of the Greenbelt North Woods allows multiple habitats to exist in close proximity.

pinkster azalea (*Rhododendron periclymenoides*). The bush has thick oval leaves that are 2–4 inches long. The leaf is similar in shape to blueberry's smaller leaf and to mountain laurel's larger leaf. In April, the pink flowers grow in clusters at the end of branches. In autumn, the brown seed pod splits open and can remain on the plant in winter. The author has found only a few pinkster azaleas in the North Woods: on the summit and northern slope of Blueberry Hill. LORE: Pinkster azalea's name may have originally been "Pinxter," which refers to its bloom time rather than its bloom color. Pinxter is the Dutch word for Pentecost, which occurs 50 days after Easter, i.e., sometime in May or June (MacKay 2013, pg. 99). This species is a member of the heath family.

blueberry (*Vaccinium* spp.). There are likely more than one species of blueberry bush growing in the Greenbelt North Woods. It can be difficult to distinguish these species from each other or from several other closely related bushes. These species are all in the heath family, and specifically, in the genera *Vaccinium* or *Gaylussacia*. For example, Greenbelt naturalists report that huckleberry and deerberry grow in the North Woods. All of these species have small oval leaves with smooth edges. The leaves are generally less than 2 inches long. In spring, the white five-petaled flower droops below the stem. The zigzaggy twigs of blueberry bushes are noticeably thinner than the twigs of other bushes like pinkster azalea and mountain laurel.

spicebush (*Lindera benzoin*). In April, the small yellow flower (3/8 inch across) emerges from a spherical bud. The leaf is oval, has a smooth edge, and has a blunt or elongated tip. In autumn, the bush has somewhat elongated bright-red berries. Most spicebushes in the Greenbelt North Woods are 5–10 feet tall and have a main stem about 1 inch in diameter. A grove of spicebushes can be found near the junction of Goddard Branch with the smaller stream that parallels Northway Road. Spicebushes can also be found where Canyon Creek enters the Beltsville Agricultural Research Center. SIMILAR SPECIES: Spicebush's leaf shape and growth form resemble those of a black gum sapling (pg. 62). Many trees and bushes have small, circular dots scattered over their bark, but the bark dots of spicebush are somewhat more raised and prominent than average. These dots are called lenticels, and they help the living tissue under the bark to exchange gases with the atmosphere.

partridge berry (*Mitchella repens*). This native ground-cover plant has pairs of small circular leaves that are somewhat triangular (1/4 to 1/2 inch long). The leaves remain green on the plant, year round. The leaf has white veins and is dark green and thick. In these ways, partridge berry's leaf resembles the much larger leaf of English ivy. In May, partridge berry has pairs of white trumpet-shaped flowers (1/2 inch long), and in winter, pairs of red berries, a few of which may stay on the plant until spring. Partridge berry remains within an inch of the ground. Given time, partridge berry can cover patches of the forest floor.

periwinkle (*Vinca minor*). This invasive ground-covering vine has pairs of thick oval leaves arranged on opposite sides of the stem. The leaf has a smooth edge. In April, the pink-violet flower has pinwheel-like petals. In autumn, the plant has brown seed pods. ECOLOGY: Periwinkle does not climb, but it can carpet the forest floor and crowd out native plants. While it was introduced to the US back in the 1700s (as a landscaping plant), it is still does not have enough natural predators and pests to restrict its growth. For this reason, periwinkle remains an invasive species today (Swearingen et al. 2010). There is a large patch of periwinkle along the forest edge at Northway Road near Ridge Road.

amur honeysuckle (*Lonicera maackii*). This invasive bush has a similar leaf shape, flower shape, and berry to that of Japanese honeysuckle (see next entry). The biggest difference is that amur honeysuckle's stems are more sturdy, allowing it to take on the form of a large bush or small tree.

SIMILAR SPECIES: Amur honeysuckle has bright-red to dark-red berries that are 1/4 inch in diameter. In contrast, tatarian honeysuckle (*Lonicera tatarica*) has orange or bright-red berries that are up to 1/2 inch in diameter. Unlike tatarian honeysuckle, amur honeysuckle has bark that splits into long, narrow, vertical strips. During 2015–2017, A. Morton Thomas and Associates (AMT) assessed the health of the city-owned portion of the Greenbelt North Woods. AMT claimed to have found tatarian honeysuckle here, but people familiar with this forest suspect that AMT actually encountered amur honeysuckle.

Japanese honeysuckle (*Lonicera japonica*). This invasive, climbing vine has pairs of oval leaves, ⚬⚬⚬. Each leaf has a smooth edge and pointed tip. When it finds a support such as a bush or tree, it may climb, cover, and smother that plant. In May, the trumpet-shaped white or yellow flower has fused petals that form a upper and lower "lip." In Autumn, the plant has bright-red to dark-purple berries. The plant was introduced to the US in 1806 (Swearingen et al. 2010).

barberry; Japanese barberry (*Berberis thunbergii*). This invasive bush has comma-shaped leaves that grow in a whorls of three to five leaves. The leaf has a smooth edge and is 1/2 to 1 inch long. The thorns along the branches are needle-like and straight and appear individually or in pairs. In spring, bell-shaped flowers dangle below the stem. The flower is small and may be either pale white, white-green, or white-yellow. In autumn, the leaf may turn orange-red, and red berries ripen that are about twice as long as they are wide (3/8 inch long). Some berries may remain on the bush until spring. Barberry is common along Goddard Branch and the smaller stream that parallels Northway Road.

Fruit (above). Main stem of mature plant (left). Back of fruit (below right). Unripe fruit (bottom right).

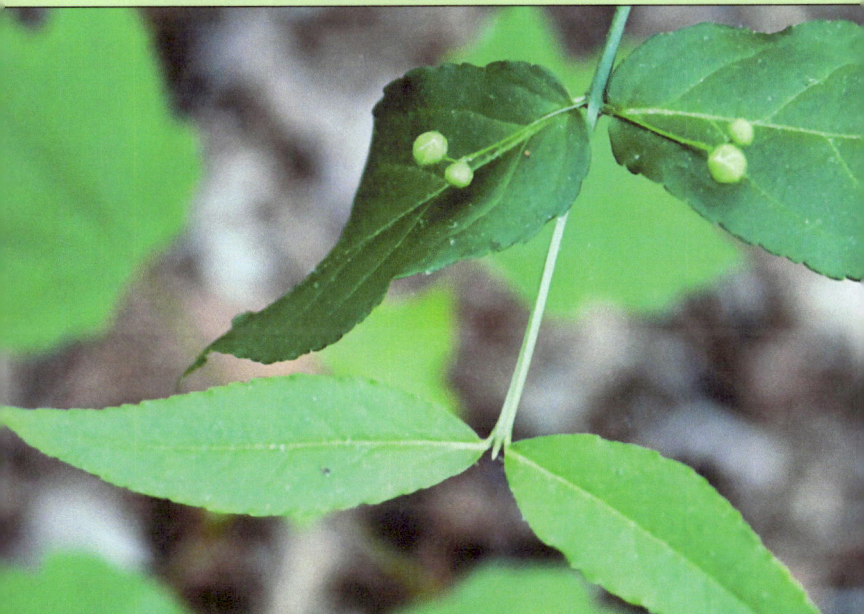

Stem, leaves, and flower buds (above). Flower (left). Twig with bud (right).

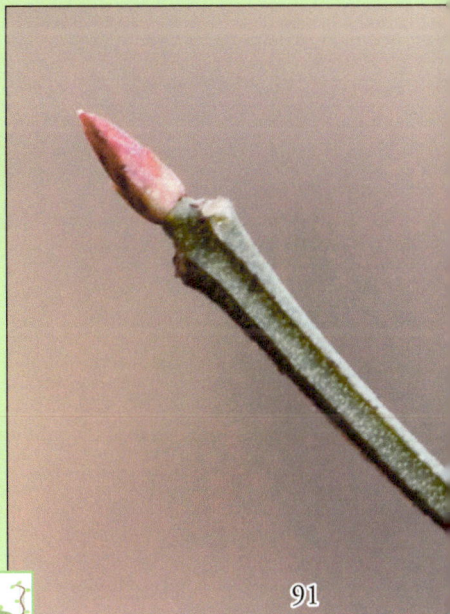

Leaves (above). Twig with buds and corky wings (below). Twig with corky wings (bottom).

blackhaw viburnum

94   ROUGH-EDGED LEAVES

ROUGH-EDGED LEAVES

bittersweet

Leaves (above). Mature stem (left). Young stems (right).

Pair of leaves (above). Cluster of flowers (below).

ROUGH-EDGED LEAVES

arrowwood viburnum

Flowers and flower buds (above). Berries (left). Main stem (right).

99

strawberry bush; hearts-a-bursting (*Euonymus americanus*). This bush has pairs of opposite leaves, that are oval with fine teeth. The leaf may be twice as long as it is wide, and occasionally even narrower. In May, the plant has pairs of green-white flowers, each flower laying on the middle of a leaf. Strawberry bush gets its name from its unusually shaped seed capsule that—if you use your imagination—looks like a strawberry. The capsule is bumpy and green when unripe and pink when ripe. In September, the capsule opens up to reveal berry-like spheres inside it. Technically, the red "berries" are actually arils, which is the term for a fleshy structure that only partially encloses a plant's seed.

LORE: Deer particularly like to eat the leaves and young twigs of this plant (Wikipedia, *Euonymus americanus*). If the deer population gets out of control in the Greenbelt North Woods, then this native species could be wiped out. As it is, the author has found only a few strawberry bushes scattered throughout the 200-acre forest.

burning bush; winged euonymus (*Euonymus alatus*). This invasive bush is called "burning bush" because of its bright-red fall foliage or "winged euonymus" because of the cork-like wings that grow along its twigs. The leaves are oval with a rough edge growing in pairs on opposite sides of the twig. This shape and arrangement of leaves is similar to that of other *Euonymus* species in the Greenbelt North Woods. The fruit is similar to that of strawberry bush. Patches of burning bush are found in the swampy land along the stream valley between Northway Road and Blueberry Hill.

wintercreeper; climbing euonymus (*Euonymus fortunei*). This invasive plant can take the form of a bush or a climbing vine. It has pairs of oval dark-green leaves, about 2 inches long. The leaf has a bright-white central vein, a slightly jagged edge, and a blunt point. The leaf's widest point is toward the base, making the leaf somewhat egg shaped, ⬭. The fruit has a similar shape to that of strawberry bush and burning bush, but wintercreeper fruit has a white-colored seed capsule.

SIMILAR SPECIES: Wintercreeper leaves are somewhat like those of partridge berry (pg. 87), except larger, longer, and slightly ragged along the edges. Wintercreeper leaves are not as narrow as periwinkle leaves (pg. 88).

LORE: Wintercreeper is native to Asia and is classified as invasive in the Eastern US. Nonetheless, wintercreeper, at this time, is fairly rare in the Greenbelt North Woods. Even though wintercreeper was introduced to the US long ago (in the 1880s), the species is still invasive today, being able to crowd out native undergrowth and to smother trees (Swearingen et al. 2010).

Wintercreeper is one of several plants named after Robert Fortune (1812–1880) who was famous for introducing various Asian plants to Europe and the US. Mr. Fortune also stole tea plants from China in violation of Chinese law in an effort help the British empire expand tea cultivation in India (Wikipedia, Robert Fortune).

blackhaw viburnum (*Viburnum prunifolium*). This bush has short oval leaves with a fine-toothed edge. The leaf resembles that of cherry and other fruit trees in the *Prunus* genus, hence blackhaw viburnum's scientific name *prunifolium*. In April, young leaves are green with red along their edge. Also in April, the small four-petaled white flowers are arranged in a flat circular cluster that is about 4 inches across. The flower clusters resemble those of arrowwood viburnum (pg. 103), which blooms in May. The blue-black drupe (a fruit with a stone at its center) is 1/2 inch in diameter and hangs from branches in autumn and winter. Blackhaw viburnum's native range is limited, going from Maryland west to the Mississippi River. It prefers sun, such as at the edge of the forest.

forsythia (*Forsythia*). In March, the bright-yellow flower has four narrow, yellow petals and blooms before the leaves come out. The leaf is oval and pointed at both ends and has a serrated edge everywhere except at its base. The seed pod is brown, fig shaped, and splits open starting from its tip to resemble an open beak. LORE: Forsythia is native to Asia or Europe, but it is not invasive in the Eastern US. Forsythia is named after the William Forsyth (1737–1804), a gardener and the founder of England's Royal Horticultural Society (Wikipedia, William Forsyth, horticulturist).

sweetpepperbush; summersweet (*Clethra alnifolia*). This bush has oval leaves with a pointed tip and fine teeth. The small white flowers form columns an inch wide and 5 inches long. The common name comes from the sweet smell of the flowers and from the green-tan seed capsules. These capsules somewhat resemble peppercorns, the spice that one grinds in pepper grinders. Sweetpepperbush prefers moist soil along streams or lakes.

bittersweet (*Celastrus orbiculatus*). An invasive vine that twists around trees to climb them, eventually strangling and killing the tree. Once a bittersweet stem grows about 1/2 inch thick, its bark has a pattern of perforations and small knobs. In autumn, a yellow spherical fruit develops that, in December, opens to reveal a red interior. The leaf is oval or circular with a jagged edge. Bittersweet is present on both banks of the Goddard Branch floodplain within the Greenbelt North Woods. **LORE:** Bittersweet was introduced from Asia to the US in the 1860s as foliage for making Christmas wreathes (MacKay 2013, pg. 273; Swearingen et al. 2010). Sometimes the plant is called Asian bittersweet or Oriental bittersweet to distinguish it from a rare native species, American bittersweet (*C. scandens*) that is not found in the Greenbelt North Woods. American bittersweet has narrow leaves, unlike the Asian bittersweet. The bittersweet family (Celastraceae) also includes strawberry bush, burning bush, and winter-creeper (see the earlier entries in this section).

arrowwood viburnum (*Viburnum dentatum*). This bush has pairs of leaves that each have a flat base, a pointed tip, and wide, pointed teeth. In May, the flower is small with five white petals. The flowers are arranged in flat-topped clusters several inches across. In September, the red berries are similarly arranged in a cluster. In the Greenbelt North Woods, many arrowwood viburnum bushes are 5–10 feet tall. As is true with many bushes, arrowwood viburnum will grow in the forest interior but prefers the more sunny forest edge. **LORE:** The name "arrowwood" comes from the plant's characteristic that its main branches grow thin, long, and straight, like the shaft of an arrow.

devil's walking stick

Doubly compound leaves (above). Thorns surrounding a leaf scar (below).

Compound leaves (above). Hairy stem climbing a tree trunk (below).

Virginia creeper

Leaf, stem, and aerial root (above). Leaf (below).

107

Flower (above). Compound leaf (left). Stem with thorn (right).

COMPOUND LEAVES

wine raspberry

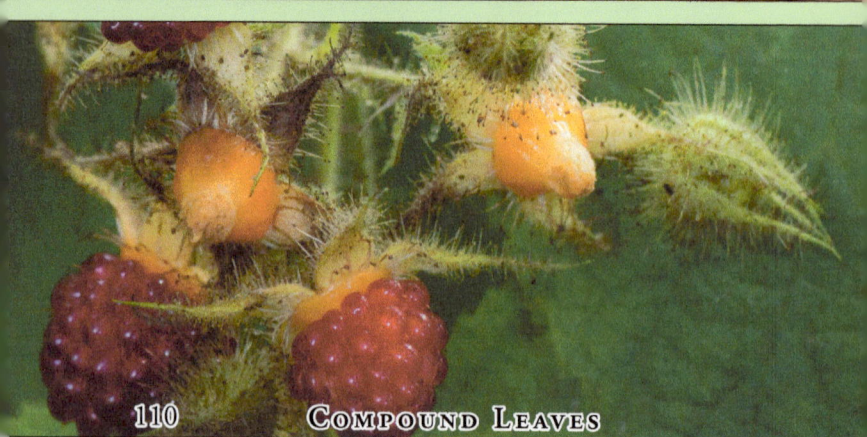

COMPOUND LEAVES

wine raspberry

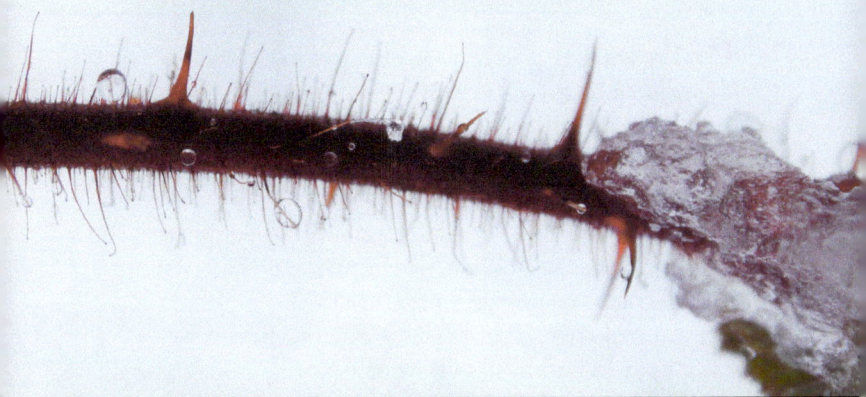

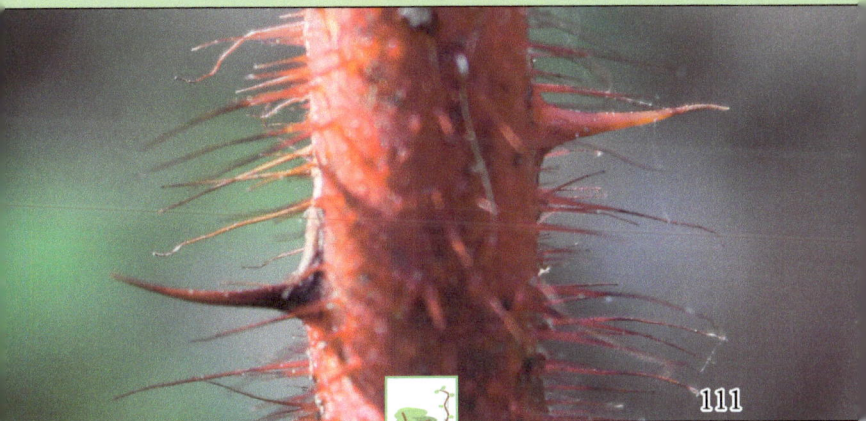

devil's walking stick (*Aralia spinosa*). This bush is identifiable by the ring of thorns around each leaf scar. Individual thorns are scattered randomly along the trunk. The bush has large double-compound leaves, i.e., the main leaf stem splits into sub-stems, which in turn bear leaflets, ⚛. The overall length of the double-compound leaf is 1–4 feet. The individual leaflets are oval, 2–5 inches long and have a flat base, pointed tip, and toothed edge. The species is rare but present in several places within the Greenbelt North Woods as well as in the adjacent Beltsville Agricultural Research Center (Terrell et al. 2000) and the nearby Patuxent Wildlife Research Refuge (Hotchkiss and Stewart 1979).

Chinese wisteria (*Wisteria sinensis*). This invasive, climbing vine has compound leaves with 9–13 leaflets. The leaflets are arranged in pairs on either side of the leaf stem, plus one leaflet sticking out of the end of the leaf stem. When lacking any supports, Chinese wisteria will take the form of a small bush, several feet high. When it finds an object to climb, Chinese wisteria will take the form of a climbing vine, wrapping counterclockwise around the support. The flowers may be white, blue, or violet, and they form hanging clusters a foot long. Wisteria's flower clusters can been seen along Maryland's highways in spring, but some wisteria in the Greenbelt North Woods has bloomed in August. LORE: The individual flowers and the seed pods resemble those of peas, which makes sense because wisteria is a member of the pea family (Fabaceae). Wisteria smothers trees and native undergrowth. A wisteria thicket covers several acres of the North Woods near 12 Court, Plateau Place.

poison ivy (*Toxicodendron radicans*). A climbing vine with sets of three leaves that have ragged edges and sometimes a shiny surface or red coloring. When the vine reaches a support (such as a nearby tree), it will climb. Once it starts climbing, the vine will produce small, white, five-petaled flowers in May. White spherical berries ripen in autumn. When climbing a tree trunk, a poison ivy stem may grow several inches thick and be completely covered with fine hair that is several inches long. WARNING: Oil in the leaf, stem, and roots can cause severe skin irritation that may require medical treatment. Teach children the rhyme "leaves of three, let it be," and help them learn to identify poison ivy. LORE: Poison ivy is native throughout the eastern US and Canada, and so by definition, it is not invasive here.

Virginia creeper (*Parthenocissus quinquefolia*). This climbing vine has compound leaves composed of five leaflets joined at their base. The leaflets have a ragged, toothed edge and sometimes a reddish color reminiscent of poison ivy. On its own, Virginia creeper's stems are too weak to rise more than a foot aboveground, but if the vine finds a tree or other support, it will climb using small areal roots with adhesive pads. In spring, the flowers are small and green. In autumn, the berries are 1/4 inch in diameter and dark blue-purple. LORE: The berries are poisonous to humans. Then again, it is a good idea to assume that all berries in the wild are poisonous unless you are very sure of the plant. The Latin name *quinquefolia* literally means "five leaved."

multiflora rose (*Rosa multiflora*). An invasive, climbing vine or bush with compound leaves usually with five leaflets. The leaflets have a ragged edge. The stem is armed with sharp, strong thorns capable of tearing clothes and puncturing skin. The thorns are usually green or bone white, while the stem is typically green or reddish green. When multiflora rose finds a support, such as a nearby tree, it climbs and smothers the tree. When growing without any support, multiflora rose forms a dense, almost impenetrable thicket. In spring, the flower is white and five-petaled like other members of the rose family, such as blackberry and cherry (next entry and pg. 60). In autumn, the fruit is a small, red sphere called a rose hip.

SIMILAR SPECIES: The thorns of multiflora rose can be bone white, unlike the multi-colored thorns of common greenbrier (pg. 120) and the reliably red thorns of wine raspberry (pg. 115).

LORE: In 1866, multiflora rose was introduced to the US. In the 1930s, the US Soil Conservation service promoted the species as a living fence to confine livestock (Swearingen et al. 2010). Later, authorities realized that multiflora rose could take over the land-scape, crowding out native species. Since about 2010, a naturally occurring rose-rust fungus (*Phragmidium rosae-multiflorea*) has spread on the East Coast that specifically attacks multiflora rose (Yun 2019). This fungus causes rose rosette disease, a disease that may kill enough bushes to eliminate multiflora rose's invasive tendency (Hartzler 2019).

blackberry (*Rubus*). A thorn bush with compound leaves that each have three leaflets. The flower has five white petals that resemble those of other members of the rose family (Rosaceae). SIMILAR SPECIES: Blackberry has smaller thorns than multiflora rose and lacks the red stem and hairs of wine raspberry. Blackberry leaves, in groups of three, tend to be all the same size, unlike wine raspberry, whose terminal leaf is larger than its two other leaves. It is difficult to distinguish blackberry species from each other and from dewberry species such as northern dewberry (*Rubus flagellaris*). LORE: Some blackberry species are native to the Eastern US and some are not.

wine raspberry; wineberry (*Rubus phoenicolasius*). A thorn bush with compound leaves that each have three leaflets. The middle leaflet is often larger than the other two leaflets. Wine raspberry's immature berries are covered completely in a red-brown leaf-like covering called a "calyx." In July, the mature berries are red, edible, and resemble commercially grown raspberries. SIMILAR SPECIES: Wine raspberry can be distinguished from other brambles by the fact that wine raspberry has bright-red twigs that are covered in red hairs and a scattering of red thorns. LORE: Wine raspberry was introduced to North America in 1890 by raspberry breeders searching for good rootstock (Swearingen et al. 2010). Sources disagree about whether wine raspberry has become naturalized (and poses no threat to native flora) or whether it is invasive (and could crowd out native species). The Latin name *phoenicolasius* refers the red color of the stems, hairs, and thorns.

maple-leaved viburnum

Flower cluster (above). Leaves (below).

wild grape

Three-lobed leaf (above). Main stem (left). Spade-shaped leaf (right).

117

common greenbrier

Radial Leaf Veins

cat greenbrier

English ivy

119

The bushes and vines in this section have a specific pattern to the veins within their leaves. Specifically, their leaves have three to five veins that radiate from a point at the base of the leaf.

maple-leaved viburnum (*Viburnum acerifolium*). This native bush has pairs of leaves that resemble red maple leaves (three lobes and a toothed edge). The bush is rather small, often just 1–4 feet tall. In spring, the flower is similar to that of arrowwood viburnum (pg. 103). In autumn, the bush has dark blue-purple berries. Maple-leaved viburnum is much rarer in the Greenbelt North Woods than is arrowwood viburnum.

wild grape (*Vitis*). This climbing vine has a range of leaf shapes. On the same vine, some leaves may be heart shaped with large teeth and an elongated tip while other leaves may have three deep lobes. Sometimes tendrils emanate from the point where the leaf stem meets the main stem. These tendrils help the vine climb. The leaf veins start from a single point at the base of the leaf. Several species of grape are native to the Eastern US. SIMILAR SPECIES: Porcelainberry (*Ampelopsis brevipedunculata*) is an invasive vine leaves that look similar to wild grape's. LORE: Most of the grape vines along Northway road are just a few feet tall, while deeper in the North Woods, a few grape vines are more mature. The stem of a mature grape vine can be several inches in diameter at ground level, and it can dangle several feet away from the tree trunk. The main stem can extend 20 feet or more upward before making contact with the trunk of the tree that it is climbing.

common greenbrier (*Smilax rotundifolia*). This thorny vine has leaves that grow on alternate sides of the green stem. The leaf is widest toward the leaf base rather than being perfectly oval. The leaf veins run parallel to the edge of the leaf, . The stem is typically 1/8–1/4 inch thick. Occasionally, one will see a pair of thin tendrils (≥4 inches long) sprouting from the base of a leaf. Half-inch-long thorns grow perpendicular to the stem. As they mature, the thorns stop being green and start having a "candy corn"-like coloring: black at the tip, a section of red, a section of white, and last a section of green next to the stem. Common greenbrier will climb a tree if one is handy, but otherwise, it takes the form of a free standing bush. The criss-crossing stems can form a thicket that is difficult to walk through. In the autumn, the blue-purple berries are similar to blueberries in shape, size, and color.

LORE: Common greenbrier is native to Maryland, and therefore, it cannot be classified as invasive here. Some people mistakenly think that common greenbrier is invasive because it forms thickets. Common greenbrier, however, does not crowd out other undergrowth or smother trees.

cat greenbrier (*Smilax glauca*). This vine is a diminutive version of common greenbrier. Cat greenbrier's thorns are thin hooks about 1/4 inch long, which is less than half as long as common greenbrier's thorns. Cat greenbrier has green stems that are less than half as thick as common greenbrier's. Cat greenbrier stays within a foot or two of the ground while common greenbrier can climb 20 feet high. Cat greenbrier has narrower leaves than common Greenbrier. Cat greenbrier's leaves are about twice as long as they are wide. Cat greenbrier has similar blue-purple berries to those of common greenbrier.

English ivy (*Hedera helix*). This invasive vine can smother trees, bushes, and ground-cover plants. When it finds a tree, English ivy climbs using aboveground roots called "aerial rootlets." The leaf has a heart-shaped base and 3–5 shallow lobes with a vein radiating from a point at the leaf base. The berry is blue-black and spherical with a dark, circular cap on one end.

SIMILAR SPECIES: There are three species of tree-climbing vines that you may see in the Greenbelt North Woods that can reach high into a tree and have a brown bark-covered stem that can be an inch or more in diameter. These three species may have no leaves at eye-level, yet can be distinguished. Suspect poison ivy if the vine stem hugs the tree trunk and is covered, all around, in inch-long hairs. Suspect English ivy if the vine stem hugs the tree trunk and has hairs only on the side where it touches the trunk. Suspect wild grape if the vine stem hangs from a high branch and is several feet away from the tree trunk at eye level.

LORE: English ivy is native to Europe and Asia. The species remains invasive in North America even though it was introduced centuries ago, in the 1700s (Swearingen et al. 2010). English ivy leaves have a thick waxy coating that makes the plant difficult to kill with herbicides. English ivy gets its water and nutrients from the ground, while its aerial rootlets merely enable the plant to climb.

Opposite: An ailanthus webworm (*Atteva aurea*) on a thistle bloom at the sunny edge of the forest bordering the Northway athletic fields. Ailanthus webworm is native to Florida, and it feeds on tree of heaven (*Ailanthus altissima*), which is an invasive tree species in Maryland.

3

Wildflowers

This chapter describes wildflowers and other plants that are a foot or two tall, that produce seeds, and that lack a woody stem or bark. You might call this category of plants the "non-woody seed-bearing plants," and a more technical term would be "herbaceous spermato-phytes." In this chapter, the plants are grouped by their overall growth form, whether it be bushy, vine-like, or otherwise. Relegated to the next chapter are plants like ferns and mosses that produce spores instead of seeds.

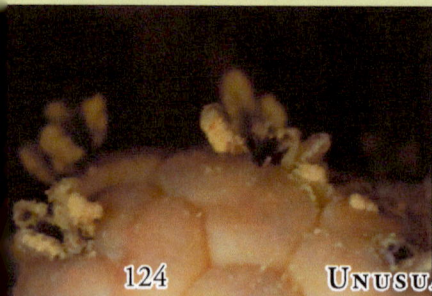

UNUSUAL FORM

skunk cabbage

← 24 inches →|

Fruit (opposite top). Flower (opposite bottom). Leaf, 1/5× life-size (above). Flower inside spathe (below).

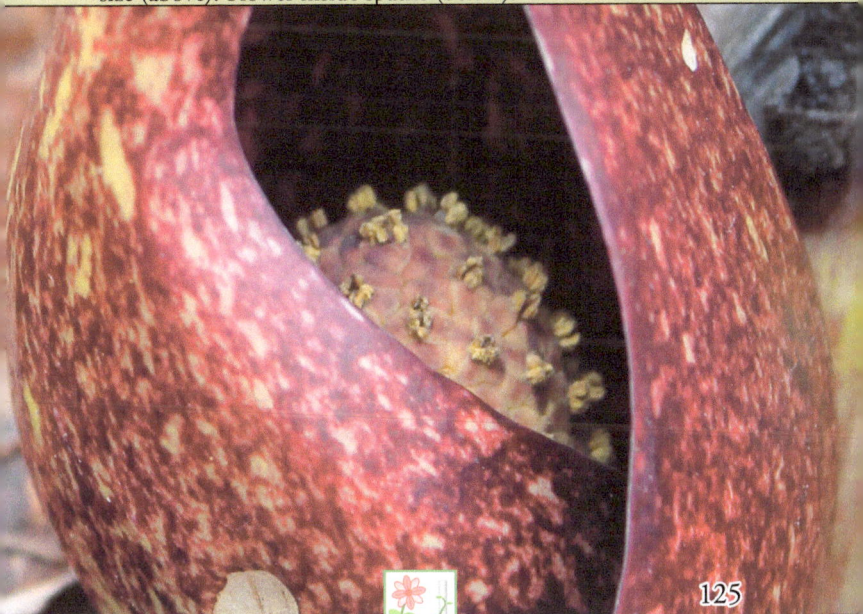

mayapple

Flower, 2× life-size (above). Leaf (below and opposite top). Flower bud, 2× life-size (opposite left) and immature fruit (opposite right).

pink lady's slipper

Typical plant, 1/2× life-size (above). Small plant, 2× life-size (below).

2× life-size

skunk cabbage (*Symplocarpus foetidus*). In February, the tiny flowers bloom on the surface of a golf-ball-sized object called a spadix. The ball is partially enclosed in a red tepee-shaped leaf-like covering about 6 inches tall, which is called a spathe. The leaves emerge in March, and they growing until they are a foot or two long by early summer. By September, the leaves wither away, and during winter, a black 2-inch-diameter fruit matures. Skunk cabbage plants may cover acres of moist, swampy land, such as along the Goddard Branch floodplain within the Greenbelt North Woods. LORE: Skunk cabbage's large leaf makes it well adapted to shady conditions. The plant's common name derives from the idea that its leaves smell bad if bruised and from the leaves' resemblance to cabbage leaves.

mayapple (*Podophyllum peltatum*). The leaf is shaped like an umbrella. The plant can have either one leaf on a vertical stem or two leaves, one at either end of a Y-shaped stem. In early summer, a plant with a Y-shaped stem will grow a 2-inch-across short-lived white flower at the branch point of the Y. The flower develops into a yellow-green fruit that is 1/2 to 2 inches long. The plant prefers shade and moist soil. LORE: Mayapple is categorized as a "spring ephemeral," which means that it flowers in spring, its roots persist for years, and its entire aboveground presence wilts away and disappears by autumn each year. Mayapple's name comes from the fact that it blooms in May with a flower that is shaped like an apple blossom. The plant's name is pronounced like the month, as in "May apple."

pink lady's slipper (*Cypripedium acaule*). Two leaves grow from the ground. A flower stalk ends in a single flower whose petals are shaped like a pair of slippers. The oval leaf has veins that run parallel to the side of the leaf, . The plant prefers dry, well-drained soil. It is rare in the Greenbelt North Woods and throughout the US East Coast.

Lore: Pink lady's slipper is in the orchid family (Orchidaceae) and is the state flower of New Hampshire. Like many orchids, pink lady's slipper depends on mycorrhizal (pronounced: mike´-oh-rise´-all) fungus in the soil to survive. For this reason, the plant is both extremely difficult to grow in gardens and also slow to spread in forests.

Meanwhile, Maryland's wild orchids are in decline due to construction on woodlands, overgrazing by deer, and encroachment by invasive species (DNR 2019; Knapp and Wiegand 2014). Some Greenbelt residents are so protective of the orchids in the North Woods that they are wary of the public knowing what species grow here, let alone their location. Most of the Greenbelt North Woods is part of the Greenbelt Forest Preserve where City Code prohibits the damaging or removing of any plant without authorization.

This field guide includes photos of three orchid species: pink lady's slipper, cranefly orchid (pg. 147), and rattlesnake orchid (pg. 147). Members of the town's naturalist club, Greenbelt Biota, have identified two other orchid species within the Greenbelt North Woods: green wood orchid (*Platanthera clavellata*) and large whorled pogonia (*Isotria verticillata*).

jack-in-the-pulpit (*Arisaema triphyllum*). Like skunk cabbage, jack-in-the-pulpit grows its flower within a leaf-like cover. The stem of jack-in-the-pulpit has a Y-shape with the vertical stem splitting in two about 1 foot aboveground. In April, a flower forms at the split. The leaves appear in spring, three leaves at either end of the Y-shaped stem. The flower lasts through much of the summer. A tight cluster of red, poisonous berries is present in August, reminiscent of an oversized, lopsided raspberry. The plant prefers moist soil. **LORE:** Jack-in-the-pulpit and skunk cabbage are in the arum family (Araceae). Both species have a large, leaf-like "hood" that covers the flower. This hood is called a spathe. Within this cover, the spherical or elongated structure on which the flowers grow is called a spadix.

Indian pipe; ghost plant (*Monotropa uniflora*). This plant has a white vertical stalk with leaf-like scales flat against the stalk. The last inch of the stalk curves back down toward the ground and terminates in a sterile flower about 1 inch long. **LORE:** Even though it is pale like a mushroom, Indian pipe nonetheless belongs to the plant kingdom. It is a member of the heath family (Ericaceae), the same family that contains blueberry, azalea, and mountain laurel. Indian pipe lacks chlorophyll, and so cannot produce its own food from sunlight. Instead, Indian pipe is a parasite that feeds off the community of fungi associated with healthy tree roots.

tall meadow rue

Leaves life-size (above). Flowers 4× life-size (left) and 3× life-size (right).

BUSHY FORM

columbine

dove's foot cranesbill

actual
size

BUSHY FORM

tick trefoil

Leaves (above). Seed pod (left). Flower (right).

tall meadow rue (*Thalictrum polygamum* also known as *Thalictrum pubescens*). A branching stem carries sets of three leaves. Each leaf has three shallow lobes and is 1–3 inches long. In June, the spherical flower is made up of thin white rays, each capped with a yellow dot. The flower is approximately 1/2 inch across. The plant prefers moist soil.

columbine; common columbine (*Aquilegia vulgaris*). The branching stem carries leaves in sets of three, each with three deep lobes. In April, the purple flower is made up of multiple trumpet-like funnels. This European species may be present in the Greenbelt North Woods because it escaped from the yards of nearby homes on Plateau Place.

dove's foot cranesbill (*Geranium molle*). The branching stem carries leaves that are deeply lobed and approximately round with tiny hairs on the upper surface. The flower has five pink, notched petals. The plant blooms in April, and it prefers moist soil.

small white aster; smooth white oldfield aster (*Symphyotrichum racemosum* formerly known as *Aster racemosus*). In September, this aster blooms with daisy-like flowers, each about 1/2 inch across. The 15–25 petals are white, and the yellow center of the flower is composed of 10–20 disk florets. When growing in the forest, the plant is several feet long and spindly. When growing in a meadow, the plant is quite bushy and can fill a cubic yard with branches, leaves, and hundreds of flowers. SIMILAR SPECIES: Several other similar-looking aster species grow in sunny places in Greenbelt but are not pictured in this field guide. For example, the spring-blooming daisy fleabane

(*Erigeron strigosus*) is found growing wild at the edge of lawns. Compared with small white aster, daisy fleabane has many more petals on its 1/2-inch-diameter flower (40–100 petals). **LORE:** A characteristic of species in the aster family is that what looks like a flower is actually a cluster of diminutive flowers called "florets."

tick trefoil, naked-flowered (*Desmodium nudiflorum*). The plant has two-inch-long oval leaves in sets of three connected to a minimally-branched main stem. While the tip of the leaf is slightly elongated, the tip is rounded off rather than ending in a sharp point. The stems of the plant are thin, with pink flowers growing along their length. Tick trefoil grows from seed each year and lacks woody stems. It grows near streams. Tick trefoil belongs to the pea family.

SIMILAR SPECIES: Tick trefoil has leaves that closely resemble those of hog peanut (*Amphicarpaea bracteata*), a member of the pea family that is not known to grow in the Greenbelt North Woods. The hog peanut flower can be identified by the green sheath that covers the back 1/2 inch of the flower. The tip of a hog peanut leaf ends in a sharp point, unlike tick trefoil's leaf. Hog peanut's flowers grow in a cluster at the end of the stem, rather than being distributed along the length of the stem. Last, hog peanut's seed pod is shaped like the snow pea that one finds at the grocery store, and not like the multiply-lobed seed pod of tick trefoil.

Flowers (above). Purple underside and green top of the leaf (below).

BASAL ROSETTE

Basal rosette with dark-green winter leaves and bright-green spring leaves (above). Seed ball (left). Leaf (right).

142   BASAL ROSETTE

Leaf on vertical stem (left). Leaf in basal rosette (right). Flower (below).

Leaf, 1/4 life-size (above). Flower, life-size (left). Seed pod, life-size (right).

BASAL ROSETTE

hairy bittercress

Leaves at the base of a plant (above). Flowers and seed pods (below).

yellow rocket

lesser celandine

BASAL ROSETTE

A basal rosette is a circle of leaves whose stems connect at a point on the ground. Some plants in this section also have a vertical leaf or flower stalk during part of the year.

cranefly orchid (*Tipularia discolor*). During winter and spring only, the plant consists of a rosette of leaves whose upper side is green with purple ribs and purple spots. The leaf's underside is solid purple. At some point in spring, the aboveground portion of the plant disappears. In summer, a vertical stalk grows that is topped with brown-white flowers, each 1/2 inch across. The plant is rare in the Greenbelt North Woods. LORE: MacKay (2013, pg. 19) speculates that the purple pigment on the underside of the leaf absorbs sunlight, which helps the leaf stay warm enough for photosynthesis to occur during winter.

rattlesnake orchid; rattlesnake plantain; creeping lady's tresses (*Goodyera pubescens*). The plant has a rosette of dark green leaves, each with a conspicuous web of white veins. During summer, a mature plant will grow a vertical flower stalk from the middle of the basal rosette of leaves. The plant persists year round as underground runners that occasional send up vertical flower shoots. The species is rare in the Greenbelt North Woods. LORE: Rattlesnake orchid is native to North America, Europe, Russia, and China, yet it is rare throughout its natural range.

Virginia knotweed; lance corporal; jumpseed; (*Persicaria virginiana* also known as *Polygonum virginianum*). The plant has a rosette of oval, green leaves. In spring, each leaf has a dark V-shaped

147

mark. By August, the dark mark has disappeared from the leaves, and a thin vertical stalk, 18 inches long, has emerged. The vertical stalk has tiny comma-shaped flowers every inch or so along its length. Each flower is about 1/8 inch long. **LORE:** Virginia knotweed is native to the Eastern US and belongs to the buckwheat family (Polygonaceae). The buckwheat family also includes lady's thumb (pg. 162) and mile-a-minute (pg. 170).

white avens (*Geum canadense*). In late winter and spring, the plant consists entirely of a basal rosette of leaf-bearing stems. The leaf has deeply incised lobes and is green with hints of purple-red. There are four to eight pairs of leaves on each stem plus a terminal leaf. The largest leaf on each stem is the one at the end. During summer, a branched stem grows 1–2 feet tall and has flowers and oval leaves. The flower has five white petals with a green petal-like structure (a sepal) lying behind and between the widely-spaced white petals. Each pointed-tip sepal may be as long as the rounded petal next to it. Native to the Eastern US.

garlic mustard (*Alliaria petiolata*). In early spring, the rosette is composed of heart-shaped leaves. The base of each leaf curls back around the leaf stem. Later in the year, a mature plant will send up a vertical stem topped with a cluster of small, white, four-petaled flowers. The leaves along this vertical stem have an elongated, pointed tip. **SIMILAR SPECIES:** The basal leaves of garlic mustard have a similar shape to the leaves of creeping charlie (pg. 167). **LORE:** The first record of garlic mustard in the US was in 1868 (Swearingen et al. 2010). The plant is invasive throughout the US. The name "garlic mustard" comes from the fact that the plant is in the mustard family and its leaves smell like garlic when crushed.

lesser burdock; common burdock (*Arctium minus*). The leaves in the basal rosette grow to a length of 6 inches or more and their central vein is red. During summer or autumn, thistle-like violet flowers bloom at the end of a 2–4-foot-tall stalk. The plant prefers meadows or the forest edge, but can tolerate full shade. Native to Europe.

hairy bittercress (*Cardamine hirsuta*). Like garlic mustard, hairy bittercress is a member of the mustard family and it starts as a basal rosette of leaves. The rosette is composed of compound leaves, about seven round leaflets on each leaf stem. The leaflets are in pairs increasing in size along the leaf stem, terminating with the largest leaflet, unpaired, at the end of the stem. Later in the growing season, a 6–12-inch-tall vertical flower stalk emerges from mature plants. Flowers are typical of the mustard family: small, white, and four petaled. The plant is not native to the US.

yellow rocket; common wintercress (*Barbarea vulgaris*). This member of the mustard family has a basal rosette of leaves that somewhat resembles the leaves of hairy bittercress. In spring and summer, the 2–3-foot-tall vertical flower stalk has small, yellow flowers with four petals. The seed pods are long, thin, and arched. Yellow rocket has been found along Northway Road in recent years. The species is not native to the US.

lesser celandine; fig buttercup (*Ficaria verna* also known as *Ranunculus ficaria*). During spring, this invasive plant has a cluster of leaves on the ground. The leaf is round with a smooth edge. The flower resembles an oversized bright-yellow buttercup flower. The aboveground portion of the plant is visible only between March and May, at which time it forms carpets in moist soil that can crowd out other flowers such as

Flowers (above). Leaves (below).

spring beauty

Stem with leaves and flowers (above). Flower shape is somewhat variable (below).

153

LONG CENTRAL STEM

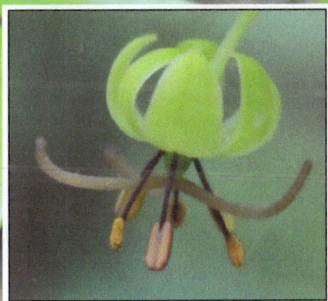

spring beauty. LORE: Lesser celandine was introduced in the US as an herb for seasoning food, and the plant escaped cultivation. The raw plant is poisonous to man and beast, and the poison is strong enough that merely touching a crushed leaf can irritate the skin.

◀ Long Central Stem

false Solomon's seal; false lily of the valley

(*Maianthemum racemosum* also known as *Smilacina racemosa*). The 1–3-foot-long arched stem is unbranched, with oval leaves hanging along its length, alternately on each side. The leaf veins are parallel to the edge of the leaf, . In May, a cluster of tiny 1/8-inch-diameter flowers is found at the end of the stem. The species is rare in the Greenbelt North Woods.

LORE: The name "Solomon's seal" may come from the fact that the plant's six-petaled flower resembles the six-pointed star that was long ago a symbol of the biblical King Solomon (Sanders 2003, pg. 81) Both smooth Solomon's seal and false Solomon's seal are in the asparagus family (Asparagaceae), as are star-of-Bethlehem (pg. 163) and Spanish bluebell (aka "wood hyacinth", *Hyacinthoides hispanica*).

SIMILAR SPECIES: False Solomon's seal has a single cluster of flowers at the end of its stem, unlike smooth Solomon's seal (next entry), which has pairs of flowers hanging along the length of its stem.

smooth Solomon's seal (*Polygonatum biflorum*).

The 1–3-foot-long arched stem is unbranched, with oval leaves hanging along its length, alternately on each side. The leaf veins are parallel to the edge of the leaf, . Both the leaves and flowers hang below the stem along the stem's full length. The flowers grow in pairs. The species is native to Europe, but not invasive in North

America. **SIMILAR SPECIES:** Another species in Europe (*Polygonatum multiflorum*) has the same common name of Solomon's seal, but its flowers come in bunches of four, not two.

yellow archangel (*Lamium galeobdolon*). This invasive plant has an unbranched stem and has oval leaves with toothed edges. In April, yellow flowers, shaped like open mouths, are arranged along a vertical stalk. A native of Europe, this sun-loving plant was found in 2017 at the forest edge along Northway Road. **LORE:** Yellow archangel is member of the mint family (Lamiaceae). Its flowers are similar in shape to those of purple dead nettle (pg. 166), another member of the mint family.

spring beauty (*Claytonia virginica*). The unbranched, vertical stem has one or two pairs of leaves shaped like fat blades of grass near the ground. The stem is about 8 inches tall. Typically one to six flowers are each attached by a short stem to the plant's main stem. The flower is 1/2 inch across and has five slender, white petals with pink or violet veins. The plant blooms before trees get their leaves each spring. **LORE:** Spring beauty is a native plant that can carpet the forest understory for acres in spring. Spring beauty is classified as a spring ephemeral because the aboveground portion of the plant disappears in summer. The species is found on both banks of Goddard Branch within the Greenbelt North Woods and along Canyon Creek near the fence for the Beltsville Agricultural Research Center. Variations exist in the flower petal's shape and color. These variations may be related to this species having a variable number of chromosomes (Griffith 2008, pg. 211). While the petals are usually white, they are sometimes pink with dark stripes.

cleavers; sticky willy (*Galium aparine*). The unbranched stem has whorls of leaves. The overall plant shape is similar to that of Indian cucumber root (see next entry). With cleavers, each whorl includes six to eight narrow 1–2-inch-long oval leaves. The stem, leaf, and seed pod have small hairs on them that cling to skin or clothing. The seed pods are spherical and about 1/4 inch in diameter. The plant grows from seed each year. Cleavers is a member of the madder family (Rubiaceae) that also includes species that produce a number of useful products: coffee (from *Coffea*) and the drugs quinine (from *Cinchona*) and ipecac (from *Carapichea ipecacuanha*).

Indian cucumber root (*Medeola virginiana*). One or more whorls of horizontal leaves grow along the length of an unbranched, vertical stem that can be 1–2 feet long. One or more flowers grow each on a short stem at the end of the plant's main stem. The flower has petals that curl back toward the stem.

sedge

lady's thumb

snowflake

Flower, 4× life-size (above). Stem with leaves and flowers (below).

The plants in this section have a grass-like form, meaning that they have long slender leaves that grow either in a tuft like lawn grass or along a vertical stem like a corn stalk. This category is somewhat subjective, and it is definitely broader than the botanical term "graminoid." The most common graminoid plants are grasses, sedges, and rushes. The following memory aid distinguishes these three kinds of plants: sedges have edges, rushes are round, and grasses have joints. The saying means that if you run you finger along the length of a sedge stem, you will feel edges, while a rush stem will feel perfectly round. Grasses tend to have knobby joints at intervals along the length of their stem.

sedge (the Cyperaceae family). The stem has "edges" or ridges along its length. Long narrow leaves grow along the length of the stem. Bladder sedge (*Carex intumescens*) has a spherical seed head composed of a dozen rounded seeds, each with a 1-inch-long spike radiating outward.

lady's thumb (*Persicaria maculosa* also known as *Polygonum persicaria*). The oval leaves each have a pointed tip, and they alternate along the vertical stem. In summer, the stem ends with a cluster of tiny, spherical pink-purple flowers. Each flower is under 1/8 inch across. The plant prefers sunny locations. LORE: Native to Europe, this wildflower long ago became common in the Eastern US.

snowflake (*Leucojum aestivum*). This plant has a tuft of grass-like leaves and a vertical, green stalk. In May, several bell-shaped flowers hang from near the top of the stalk. Each white petal has a green dot at its tip. The plant grows from a bulb. LORE: Snowflake is a native of Europe and Russia that has naturalized in the Eastern US, meaning that it survives in the wild but it does not threaten native species.

Japanese stiltgrass (*Microstegium vimineum*). This grass has leaves about 4–6 times longer than they are wide. The leaves grow along a vertical stem that can be 1–3 feet tall by the end of the summer. In recent years, this invasive grass has carpeted many acres of the Goddard Branch floodplain within the Greenbelt North Woods. The plant grows from seed each spring.

star-of-Bethlehem (*Ornithogalum umbellatum*). This plant emerges from the ground as a tuft of narrow leaves about 8–12 inches long and 1/4 inch wide. The vertical, branched stem carries flowers and additional leaves. The six-petaled flower is usually a bit less than an inch in diameter. The underside of each petal has a green stripe. On the upper side of each petal, there are two thin white lines from center to tip. The plant is native to Europe, and some authorities consider it invasive in the Eastern US.

Leaf, 2× life-size (above). Flowers (below), all approximately life-size except for bottom right.

speedwell

purple dead nettle

bugleweed

creeping charlie

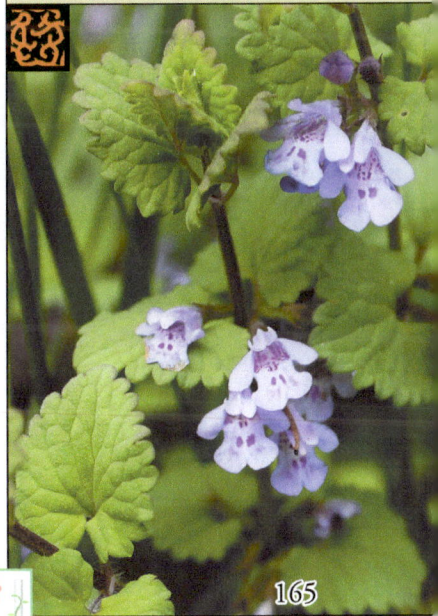

The ground-hugging non-woody plants in this section stay within about 8 inches of the ground and can form dense mats of foliage. This mat-like low growth differs from the discrete clumps of foliage of the plants described earlier in the Basal Rosette and Grass-like sections of this chapter.

common blue violet; wild violet (*Viola papilionacea* also known as *V. sororia*). Each heart-shaped leaf is a few inches long and sits at the end of its own stem (also several inches long) that emerges directly from the ground. In spring, the plant has violet- or white-colored flowers with five petals, each on its own stem that emerges from the ground. SIMILAR SPECIES: Common blue violet is one of several ground-cover plants in the Greenbelt North Woods whose leaves can be roughly described as spade shaped, ♠. Other such plants are garlic mustard (pg. 148), creeping charlie (later in this section), and lesser celandine (pg. 149). During spring, common blue violet can be easily distinguished from these other species by its flower shape. LORE: Common blue violet is the state wildflower of New Jersey.

speedwell; common field-speedwell (*Veronica persica*). The leaves are tight bundles that stay within a couple of inches of the ground. The blue flower has a yellow-white center and four petals with prominent deep-blue radial veins. In April or earlier, speedwell blooms at the edge of the Greenbelt North Woods. It is native to Eurasia.

purple dead nettle (*Lamium purpureum*). In late winter or early spring, the plant grows an 8-inch-tall vertical stalk that carries leaves and flowers. The triangular leaves are densely arranged along the length of a stem. Sometimes the uppermost leaves or the entire plant have a red blush. Starting in February, the stem also has mouth-shaped pink flowers that are interspaced among the leaves. A member of the mint family.

SIMILAR SPECIES: Another plant in the mint family with similar leaves and pink flowers is self-heal (*Prunella vulgaris*), also known as heal-all. Self-heal has flowers bunched together at the top of the stem like a miniature corncob, while purple dead nettle has flowers interspaced among its leaves. Self-heal is not pictured in this field guide because it is more likely to be found in a lawn than in the forest.

Bugleweed is another member of the mint family that grows in the Greenbelt North Woods. Bugleweed has mouth-shaped flowers that are blue-purple and its leaf has an unusual purple or bronze tinge (see next entry).

A final similar-looking member of the mint family is creeping charlie (see last entry in this section). Anita Burkam notes that bloom time can help distinguish these species, and in Maryland, it is purple dead nettle and creeping charlie in February and March, bugleweed in April and May, and self-heal in July and August.

bugleweed; ajuga (*Ajuga reptans*). In April, the plant grows an 8-inch-tall vertical stalk that carries leaves and flowers. The flower is purple blue and mouth shaped. The leaf and stem are slightly tinged with a purplish-blue color. The plant can carpet the forest floor.

creeping charlie; ground ivy (*Glechoma hederacea*). The plant has round leaves (1/2 to 1 inch across) with scalloped edges. Leaf stems may emerge directly from the ground in a disorganized mass or vertical stems may arise with multiple leaves that hug the stem. The flower is blue-violet and funnel shaped.

Stem with leaf and flower (above). Fruit (below).

wild yam

mile-a-minute

common vetch

The plant tolerates shade but prefers sun. It is well established around the municipal mulch pile next to Northway athletic fields, but it also grows within the surrounding forest. The species is not native to the US.

◀ Non-woody Vines

mock strawberry; Indian strawberry (*Potentilla indica* also known as *Duchesnea indica*). The entire vine stays within a few inches of the ground and propagates by means of runners, which are green stems that trail along the ground. The plant has sets of three leaves that have a somewhat similar shape to those of true strawberry. The flower is yellow, unlike the white flower of true strawberry. The fruit is red and similar in shape to a true strawberry. The fruit is only about 1/2 inch across, and it has tiny red seeds raised above its surface. LORE: Mock strawberry is a common plant in lawns and at the forest edge, but it is not native to North America. The *Indica* in mock strawberry's Latin name refers to the country of India. In other words, the Latin name refers to a part of the world where this species is native and the not to Native Americans.

wild yam (*Dioscorea villosa*). This climbing vine has a heart-shaped leaf. The leaf veins are sunk below the surface of the leaf, the veins originate at a point at the base of the leaf, and the veins are unbranched. In contrast, the similarly shaped leaf of the redbud tree has branched veins. Wild yam leaves grow in whorls of 3–6 leaves every foot or so along the main stem. As the summer progresses, the vertical stem elongates and becomes vine-like with minimal branching. The plant climbs by its main stem twining around objects.

mile-a-minute (*Persicaria perfoliata*). This climbing vine has triangular leaves on thin green stems. The stems are armed with thorns that are short and sharp. The plant also has 1/2-inch-across disk-shaped leaves that ring the stem. In July, the plant has light-blue spherical berries that are about the size of blueberries. This invasive annual vine forms a dense tangle several feet high along the Goddard Branch floodplain. The species was unintentionally introduced to the US by a nursery in Pennsylvania (Swearingen et al. 2010). Because mile-a-minute can aggressively take over the understory, it is sometimes called the "kudzu of the north," a nickname that may also be applied to bittersweet (pg. 102).

common vetch (*Vicia sativa*). This member of the pea family has a vertical stalk with long leaves each with a pointed tip. The stalk also carries violet-pink flowers whose shape is typical of the pea family (pg. 226). The plant grows in the meadow at the southeastern edge of the Greenbelt North Woods. While vetch is sometimes classified as an invasive plant, it cannot tolerate shade sufficiently to take over the forest understory. Some farmers grow vetch as a fodder for livestock. Vetch is native to Europe and the Middle East.

Above: The author's sons explore the Greenbelt North Woods. Clockwise from the upper left: December on Northway stream, May in a double-trunked hollow tree in the Goddard Branch floodplain, August in front of a large tulip poplar, and October at the Canyon Creek erosion gully. **Opposite:** Fan clubmoss (*Diphasiastrum digitatum*) over a bed of pincushion moss (*Leucobryum*).

172

4

Ferns, Mosses, & Clubmosses

Trees and flowers produce seeds, but ferns, mosses, and clubmosses do not. A seed includes a miniature leaf, stem, and root. A fern, moss, or clubmoss produces spores instead of seeds. A spore is a single cell that is dispersed into the wind and that can grow into a complete plant. Some seed and spore plants can also reproduce vegetatively, which means that a piece of the parent plant breaks off and becomes a separate individual.

Before wildflowers, pines, or even dinosaurs evolved, there were forests of giant ferns and clubmosses that grew at least 50 feet tall (Willis and McElwain 2014). Ferns and clubmosses were so numerous, 400 million years ago, that a thick layer of them piled up and eventually became some of today's supply of coal and natural gas.

Christmas fern

Stem and leaflets, 2× life-size (above). Underside of leaflet with spores attached (below).

New York fern

Frond (above). Underside of leaflets with disks of spores, 6×
life-size (below).

cinnamon fern

Upper side of leaflets (above). Underside of stem and leaflet with tuft of white fuzz at each junction, 5× life-size (below).

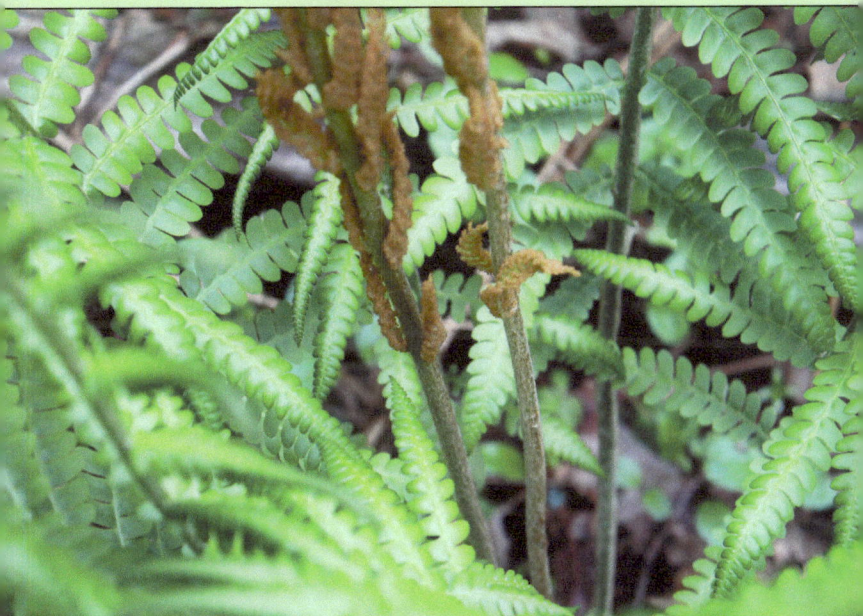

Green fronds and spore fronds (above and below left). Close up of green frond not yet uncurled (right).

hay-scented fern

rattlesnake fern

FERNS

bracken fern

The table below summaries the fern species found in the Greenbelt North Woods. Each species may be categorized by how many stems emerge from the ground and whether the leaflets connect directly to the main stem or to secondary stems. The shape of the leaflet also assists with identification. The majority of ferns in the Greenbelt North Woods are either Christmas fern, New York fern, cinnamon fern, or hay-scented fern, and their prominence is indicated in the table with ★★. Sensitive fern is less common (★), while bracket fern and rattlesnake fern are rare (**R**).

	Multiple fronds emerge from the ground	A single stem emerges from the ground
Once-compound frond	★★ Christmas fern ★ sensitive fern	
Twice-compound frond	★★ New York fern ★★ cinnamon fern ★★ hay-scented fern	**R** bracken fern **R** rattlesnake fern

Christmas fern (*Polystichum acrostichoides*). The boot-shaped leaflets attach directly to the main stems that emerge from the ground. The leaflet is approximately 2 inches long. Christmas fern is the only fern in the Greenbelt North Woods whose fronds can survive the winter. Occasionally, spores are found on the underside of the frond. LORE: Christmas fern's common name comes from the fact that it is still green at Christmastime.

New York fern (*Thelypteris noveboracensis*). The leaflet has feather-like ribs and is 2–3 times longer than it is wide. Occasionally, there are spores on the underside of the green frond. The frond narrows at both its tip and its base, which inspired the following memory aid: New York ferns, like New Yorkers, burn the candle at both ends. New York fern is common in stream valleys.

cinnamon fern (*Osmunda cinnamomea* also known as *Osmundastrum cinnamomeum*). Cinnamon fern is the largest fern in the Greenbelt North Woods. The green frond may be up to 4 feet long. For a few weeks in late spring or early summer, a spore stalk is present in the center of the ring of green fronds. The spores grow on many miniature fronds (a few inches long) that are arranged along the length of the spore stalk. Cinnamon fern is generally found on higher ground unlike other fern species that generally stay in the floodplain. Nonetheless, the exact spot where a cinnamon fern grows will have moist soil, such as in a patch of muddy ground where the water table is habitually at the surface (i.e., a "seep").

SIMILAR SPECIES: Both cinnamon fern and New York fern have similarly shaped leaflets with feather-like veins, but cinnamon fern's leaflets are larger and stouter (3/8 inch long). If you look closely at the underside of the frond, you will notice that Cinnamon fern is the only fern species in the Greenbelt North Woods that has a 1/8-inch-across tuft of white hair where each small side stem joins the main stem of the frond.

In their 2017 assessment of the Greenbelt Forest Preserve, A. Morton Thomas and Associates claimed that ostrich fern (*Matteuccia struthiopteris*) grows in the Greenbelt North Woods. Greenbelt residents familiar with the forest have never found ostrich fern here. Ostrich fern is common in North America, Europe, and Asia, and it can be easily identified in fall and winter by its brown spore stalk that resembles a long feather. The spore stalk is about 2 inches wide and several feet long. Ostrich fern's green fronds are a wider-and-longer version of the green fronds of both cinnamon fern and New York fern. Also, ostrich fern's green fronds have their widest point near their tip, while cinnamon fern fronds have their widest point near their middle or their base.

hay-scented fern (*Dennstaedtia punctilobula*). The leaflet resembles a parsley leaf. Spores are occasionally found on the underside of the frond. This fern is common in stream valley. SIMILAR SPECIES: Hay-scented fern and rattlesnake fern have similarly shaped leaflets, but only hay-scented fern has multiple fronds that emerges from the ground. The leaflet resembles a parsley leaf. Spores are occasionally found on the underside of the frond. This fern is common in stream valleys.

rattlesnake fern (*Botrypus virginianus*, previously *Botrychium virginianum*). The leaflet resembles a parsley leaf. A single, vertical, leafless stem emerges from ground, and a foot aboveground, this vertical stem divides into three small fronds. A short-lived spore stalk emerges vertically from the junction point. The plant overall is about a foot wide, which is smaller than most of the other fern species in the Greenbelt North Woods. Rare in the Greenbelt North Woods.

bracken fern (*Pteridium aquilinum*). The leaflets on the frond somewhat resemble those of Christmas fern, except that bracken fern leaflets may have two "toes," one on each side of the leaflet's base. Like rattlesnake fern, bracken fern has a single stem emerge from the ground that splits in three at a height of about 1 foot aboveground. Rare in the Greenbelt North Woods. Grows in temperate regions around the world.

sensitive fern (*Onoclea sensibilis*). The frond is webbed, and rarely over a foot long. The leaflet has a wavy edge. In late summer, a separate brown frond grows that has, along its length, countless brown spheres, 1/16 inch in diameter. These brown spheres contain spores. The common name for sensitive fern may come from the fact that this species is quick to wilt after the first frost. Rare in the Greenbelt North Woods. SIMILAR SPECIES: The green frond of sensitive fern is similar in appearance to that of the much rarer, netted chain fern (*Woodwardia areolata* also known as *Lorinseria areolata*). The distinguishing characteristic is that sensitive fern's leaflets grow in pairs on opposite sides of the main stem. In contrast, netted chain fern's leaflets alternate on either side of the main stem.

fern moss

foxtail moss

185

Leaves and spore pods, 2× life-size (above). Leaves, 5× life-size (below).

actual
size

186

MOSSES

tooth moss

Leaves and spore pods, 2× life-size (above). Leaves, 5× life-size (below).

actual
size

Entire plant, life-size (above). Clusters of leaves, 3× life-size (below).

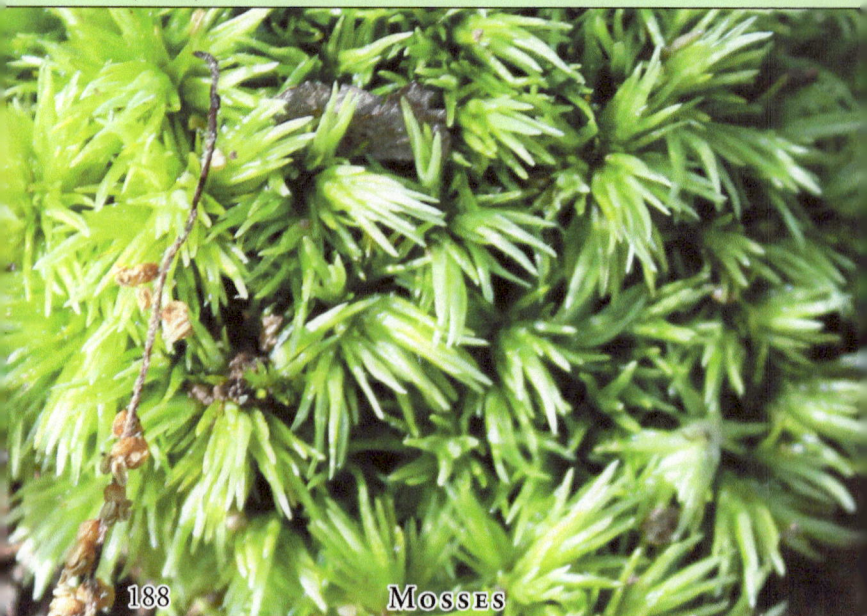

◀ Mosses

While moss can grow on bark, soil, or other surfaces, moss does not draw nutrients from the surface that it grows on. Instead moss extracts nutrients for producing food from the air around it and from raindrops that fall on it. This characteristic of moss makes it an epiphyte, a living thing that grows on the surface of a plant but is not parasitic (McKnight et al. 2013, pg. 29). The only other example of an epiphyte in this field guide is lichen (pg. 220). Moss leaves are typically just one cell thick, which makes it easier for them to absorb water and gas for photosynthesis directly from the air around them.

Moss lacks the xylem tissue that transports water and nutrients up from the ground in other plants (Willis and McElwain 2014, pg. 68). Moss also lacks the phloem tissue that transports food back down to the roots of other plants. Because it lacks xylem and phloem, moss is classified as a non-vascular plant. The first land plants to emerge from the ocean, half a billion years ago, were non-vascular too. The height that moss can grow is limited by its non-vascular nature. The thick cell walls of xylem tissue makes vascular plants rigid enough to grow more than a few inches tall, but moss lacks xylem.

Another odd thing about moss is that the green-leafy plant that we see has only a single copy of each chromosome, unlike most plants and animals. Periodically, a moss patch will grow inch-tall thin brown-tan stalks. At the top of each stalk is a tiny cylindrical spore pod. Each stalk and pod is a genetically separate individual growing on top of and drawing nutrients from the larger single-chromosome leafy-green individual that gave birth to it. The stalk and pod constitute an individual with two copies of each chromosome.

Most of the kinds of moss listed below have a

common name inspired by the shape of their leafy green structure. A 10× magnifying glass can help you see this structure.

fern moss (*Thuidium*). Fern moss gets its name from its branches resembling a fern frond in miniature.

foxtail moss (*Brachythecium*). The long, meandering stems of foxtail moss can have an appearance remi-

niscent of a braided friendship bracelet. The tiny green leaves press against the stem.

starburst moss (*Atrichum*). When viewed from above, the leaves looks like they radiate from a single point, like fireworks. **SIMILAR SPECIES**: Haircap moss (*Polytrichum* also known as *Polytrichastrum*) is a similar-looking genus to starburst moss, and both of these genera grow in the Greenbelt North Woods. Upon close inspection, haircap moss can be distinguished by the small widely-spaced teeth along the edge of its leaf.

Haircap moss showing the tiny teeth along its leaf edge. Photo enlarged 7× life-size.

tooth moss (*Plagiomnium*). The individual leaves of tooth moss somewhat resemble pointed teeth.

pincushion moss (*Leucobryum*). This moss get its name from its large-scale structure: it forms a rounded mass that can be several inches to a foot across. The

rounded mass somewhat resembles a pin-cushion, the kind that seamstresses use to store straight pins. (image credit: u-createcrafts.com)

fan clubmoss

shining clubmoss

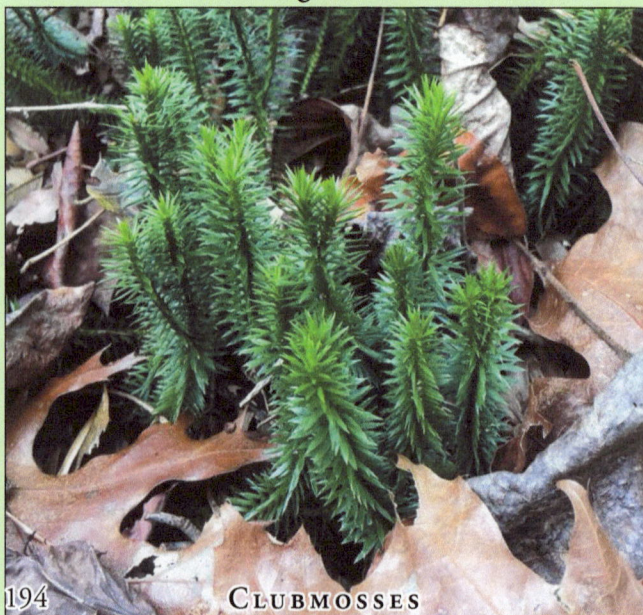

Photo credit: Catherine Plaisant

194   CLUBMOSSES

◀ Clubmosses

Clubmoss is in a separate division of the plant kingdom than is true moss (Lycopodiophyta vs. Bryophyta). This classification means that these two kinds of plant are only distantly related despite their superficial resemblance. Both clubmoss and moss are green plants with tiny leaves, and they grow within a few inches of the ground. Both clubmoss and moss produce spores rather than seeds. The internal structure of clubmoss and moss, however, differs in an important way. Clubmoss has vascular tissue for transporting water up from the ground, a characteristic that it shares with trees.

Because clubmoss is easily damaged by foot traffic, a large patch that spans an area 100 feet across or more suggests that the clubmoss has been growing mostly undisturbed for many decades. Patches this large in the Greenbelt North Woods reflect the fact that this forest has, for the most part, been left alone to mature since Greenbelt was founded 80 years ago. In a patch of clubmoss, the aboveground vertical stems are often connected underground by their roots, and they represent a single individual.

princess pine (*Lycopodium obscurum*). This clubmoss is shaped like a miniature Christmas tree and has many tiny leaves that are longer than its stem is wide. The leaves are long and narrow, approximately the shape and size of a grain of rice. The leaves are so closely spaced that most of what you see is leaf, not stem. Part of the year, princess pine will have one-to-three spore-bearing cones, each called a "strobilus." The spore cone is tan, narrow, and a few inches long. It grows vertically from the top of princess pine's central stem.

fan clubmoss, crowsfoot, running cedar
(*Diphasiastrum digitatum*). This clubmoss is shaped like
a miniature Christmas tree and has tiny leaves along its
stem. The leaves are shaped like the swept-back wings of
a supersonic jet. Part of the year, fan clubmoss will
have three-to-five spore-bearing cones. The spore
cone is tan, narrow, and a few inches long. It grows
vertically from the top of the plant's central stem. Just
below the spore cones, the green stem resembles a
miniature version of an asparagus stem.

shining clubmoss (*Huperzia lucidula*). Unlike other
clubmosses in the Greenbelt North Woods, shining
clubmoss takes the form of a unbranched vertical stem
that is several inches long. The needle-like leaves extend
horizontally away from the vertical stem. This species is
rare in the Greenbelt North Woods. Generally, this field
guide includes only plants that the author has seen and
photographed in the North Woods, but an exception
is made here for shining clubmoss. Local naturalist
Catherine Plaisant has documented the existence of
shining clubmoss along Canyon Creek and provided the
photo.

5

Fungi, Slime Molds, & Lichens

This chapter introduces an odd collection of living things that grow in the Greenbelt North Woods. They are neither plants nor animals. Instead, they are fungi, slime molds, and lichens.

The longest-lived part of a fungus is a web of white threads that grow within plant matter and that dissolve and consume that plant matter. These threads are called hyphae. The mushrooms that we buy at the grocery store are merely spore-producing bodies that hyphae gave birth to. When the cap and stem of a mushroom appears, it is evidence that, out of sight, the hyphae of two individuals of the same species have encountered each other, joined together, and enjoyed the right conditions to grow a spore-producing body.

The term "fungus" has a more precise meaning than "mushroom," because fungus always refers to the entire living thing, including the hyphae and any spore-producing body that has sprouted from the hyphae. In contrast, one must use context to guess if "mushroom" is being used as a synonym for an entire fungus or if "mushroom" refers to only part of a certain fungi: the cap and stem of the sort of fungus whose spore-pro-ducing body is this shape. A cap and stem is by no means the only possible shape for a fungus' spore-pro-ducing body, as the pictures in this chapter demonstrate. (See also Wikipedia, mushroom; Phillips 2005, pg. 6.)

DNA analysis has determined that fungi and animals are on the same branch of the biological tree of life. In other words, fungi and animals share a common ancestor, a common ancestor that is not an ancestor of plants. Fungi obviously lack the organs typical in animals, but there are intriguing similarities. In general, both fungi and animals feed off of plants while plants make their own food. Many fungi and some animals use a complex carbohydrate called chitin that is not found in plants. Chitin strengthens the cell walls of mushrooms, and in the animal kingdom, chitin is a component of fly wings and worm skins.

As for a lichen, it is actually two creatures in one. It consists of a fungus that maintains within its body a colony of algae. The algae produces food for the fungus, and the fungus provides the algae moisture and protection from the elements.

Stranger still is a slime mold, a living thing that, believe it or not, is a single cell that is large enough to be visible to the naked eye. Instead of being a plant, animal, or fungus, a slime mold is a giant cousin of the amoeba. Unless you have noticed slime molds in the forest before, the only amoebas that you have probably seen are the tiny single-cell creatures that you examined under the microscope in high-school biology.

waxy cap mushroom

russula mushroom

bonnet mushroom

funnel mushroom

UMBRELLA-SHAPED FUNGI

◀ Umbrella-shaped Fungi

A number of the boldface entries in this section and the next two sections are less precise than those elsewhere in this field guide. Rather than describe a specific species or genus, these entries describe merely a group of similar-looking species that are not necessarily closely related genetically. Waxy cap, bonnet, and funnel mushrooms are three examples of such groups.

A category of living thing is called "polyphyletic" if the category includes similar-looking species that are unrelated genetically. Resorting to polyphyletic categories is unavoidable in an introductory text on fungi. Many fungus species would be difficult to identify without destructive procedures such as harvesting the mushroom and making a spore print or examining it under a microscope. Without prior approval, harvesting from the Greenbelt Forest Preserve would violate the City Code. Information in this section comes from Wikipedia.com, mushroomexpert.com, americanmushrooms.com, and texts cited in the Reference section.

waxy cap mushroom. A category of fungi that have a cap that appears as if it has been molded out of wax. Many waxy cap fungi have gills on the underside of their cap. The cap and stem may be a translucent bright orange or yellow, as is the case for orange-gilled waxy cap (*Hygrophorus marginatus*). LORE: While the *Hygrophorus* and *Hygrocybe* genera are called the waxy cap genera, DNA analysis in recent decades has shown that some fungi with a "waxy cap" look are not closely related genetically to the rest of the waxy cap fungi (Wikipedia, Hygrophoraceae; https://www.mushroomexpert.com/hygrophoraceae.html). For example, a novice might say that chanterelle mushrooms

(*Cantharellus*) have a waxy-cap look although chante-relles fall outside of these two genera.

russula mushroom (*Russula*). Many species in the genus *Russula* have caps with a bright color on top, they have a white stem, and they have gills on the underside of their cap. The genus is quite large, containing 750 species worldwide (Wikipedia, *Russula*).

bonnet mushroom. Bonnet mushrooms, also known as fairy helmet mushrooms, tend to have a cap that is small (<1 inch across), delicate, and thin enough to be translucent. The top of the cap may have a central bump and fine radial lines going from the center to the brim of the cap. The brim may curl down when young and may be flat or curl upward when older. Examples include bleeding-foot mycena (*Mycena haematopus*), fairy-ring mushroom (*Marasmias oreades*), and Caesar's mushroom (*Amanita caesarea*) (Phillips 2005, pg. 17). LORE: Michael Kuo describes this group of fungi as including "some of the most beautiful and elegant mushrooms on Earth" (https://www.mushroomexpert.com/mycenoid.html). Many bonnet mushrooms were originally placed in the genus *Mycena*, but the genus might be reor-ganized now that DNA analysis has shown that many of the similar-looking fungi species originally placed in this genus are not closely related genetically.

funnel mushroom. Fungi described as being funnel-shaped generally have a cap whose sides curve upward like a funnel, ▼. Many of these fungi have caps with gills that continue down the side of the stem. The top of the cap may be flat for part of their lifetime. Examples include club-footed clitocybe (klie´-tass-uh-bee, *Ampulloclitocybe clavipes*), short-stemmed russula (*Russula brevipes*), and deceiving milkcap (*Lactarius deceptivus*).

Crust fungus in the genus *Biscogniauxia* (above), *Phlebia* (below left), and *Xylobolus* (below right).

turkey tail

split gill fungus

violet toothed polypore

3× life-size (above). Life-size (below)

◀ Stemless Fungi

The only characteristic that the mushrooms in this section have in common is that their cap is directly attached to the dead wood that they grow on. The cap may be a thick semicircle growing horizontally out from a vertical log, or it may be a lumpy coating that grows flat against the log. The technical term for stemless is "resupinate." Resupinate fungi are a polyphyletic group, meaning that these species are not all closely related genetically.

crust fungi (corticioid fungi). Crust fungi typically have a smooth, thin, irregularly shaped cap that is several inches across and that appears to be glued onto the surface of the log that the fungus is growing on. Crust fungi is a polyphyletic group.

Biscogniauxia: A genus of crust fungi that includes white crust fungi with black dots, such as *Biscogniauxia atropunctata* also known as *Hypoxylon atropunctatum*. When young, *B. atropunctata* is white with a slight bluish hue. This genus also includes black-colored tar fungi.

Phlebia radiata: A pale-orange crust fungus. The wrinkled surface grows outward from a central point.

Xylobolus frustulatus: A crust fungus consisting of white polygons separated by lines of black "grout." The white polygons are generally less than 1/2 inch across while the overall patch may be over a foot across.

turkey tail (*Trametes versicolor*). The cap grows directly on a dead branch. The cap is colored with concentric stripes of white, brown, or black. Looking along the edge of the cap, one can see pores on the underside. These pores enable one to distinguish turkey tail (*Trametes versicolor*) from false turkey tail (*Stereum ostrea*), which has a smooth underside. The underside pores of turkey tail identify it as a polypore fungus, the category of fungus that includes milked-white toothed polypore and violet toothed polypore (see entries below).

split gill fungus (*Schizophyllum commune*). A white or cream-colored fungi with a cap and no stem. The front edge of the cap has fuzzy hairs and the underside has gills that split in two as they approach the brim of the cap.

violet toothed polypore (*Trichaptum biforme*). The upper surface of the cap has concentric rings of alternating light and dark colors. In this regard, violet toothed polypore is very similar to turkey tail (see an earlier entry). What distinguishes violet toothed polypore is its pale-violet underside, which has a bumpy surface (i.e., "pores").

lions mane (*Hericium*). This genus contains several species with small downward-pointing white fingers that form a single large clump when mature.

milk-white toothed polypore (*Irpex lacteus*). This white or off-white fungus grows flat against a log and has tooth-like projections hanging down. The edge curls away from the log (www.mushroomexpert.com).

devil's urn

common puffball

swamp beacon

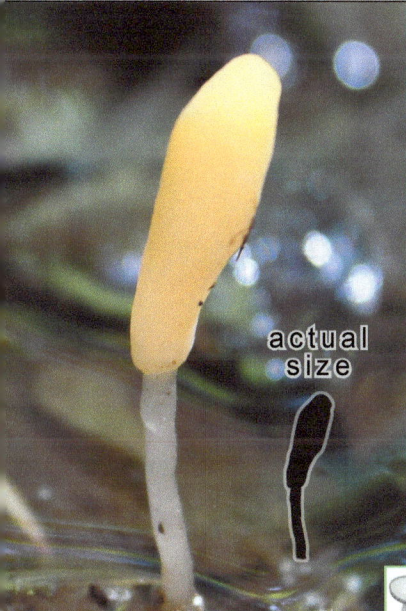

actual size

fairy fingers

life size

209

black trumpet

stinky squid

amber jelly roll

witches' butter

black jelly roll

devil's urn (*Urnula craterium*). This fungus is a kind of "cup" fungus, named after the cup-like shape of the fruiting body. For devil's urn, the cup is 1–4 inches across. It grows on dead sticks and small logs that are often buried, so the mushroom appears to be growing from the soil. The inner surface of the cup is black and smooth. The outer surface is gray or brown and may be cracked. Spores are produced along the inner surface of the cup. Devil's urn is found in America and Eurasia (www.mushroomexperts.com, Wikipedia).

common puffball (*Lycoperdon*). Puffballs are an informal category of mushroom with a ball-shaped fruiting body that, when mature, opens at the top to release spores that had been developing inside the ball. The genus *Lycoperdon* is a common genus of puffballs in the Eastern US that is characterized by small raised dots on the outside of the ball (www.mushroomexperts.com). The genus is found in America and Eurasia.

swamp beacon; match-stick fungus (*Mitrula elegans*). The aboveground portion of the fungus consists of a thin white stalk with a small yellow cap. It grows about an inch tall on decaying vegetation in shallow water. This amphibious fungus can decompose plant material in low-oxygen environments, such as occur in swamp water. In the 1970s, the US species *M. elegans* was distinguished from the similar species (*M. paludosa* also known as *M. phalloides*) that grows in Europe. Both the US and European species share the same common name, "swamp beacon."

fairy fingers (*Clavaria vermicularis*). The white vertical stalk somewhat resembles a bean sprout, the kind of sprout that you find in the grocery store's produce aisle. A fairy fingers stalk is typically unbranched, 2–5 inches tall, and 1/8 inch thick. Stalks often grow in clusters. The upper tip of the stalk can become yellowish or pale brownish, i.e., "discolored," with age. SIMILAR SPECIES: Fairy fingers (*C. vermicularis*) is always translucent white, whereas the color of a similar-looking species (*C. fragilis*) varies based on soil conditions. LORE: Also called "white spindle." Fairy fingers is a coral-type fungus, meaning that many aboveground stalks grow from a single base.

black trumpet; horn of plenty (*Craterellus fallax*). Black trumpet forms its spores on the outside of the funnel, unlike devil's urn, which forms spores on the inside of its "cup" (Phillips 2005, pg. 213).

stinky squid mushroom (*Pseudocolus fusiformis*). This fungus is identifiable by its three or four orange arms that join at their tip. The dark blobs along the inner surface of the arms are masses of spores called gleba (Phillips 2005, pg. 290). The fungus grows in soil or wood mulch.

amber jelly roll (*Exidia recisa*). A kind of jelly fungus that is light brown. As with other jelly fungi, the spores are produced on the surface.

witches' butter (*Tremella mesenterica*). A kind of jelly fungus that is translucent yellow. Also called "yellow brain" (Wikipedia, *Tremella mesenterica*). This fungus can be several inches across. It grows specifically on hardwood bark, not pine bark.

black jelly roll (*Exidia glandulosa*). A kind of jelly fungus that is extremely dark brown or black.

dog vomit slime mold

wolf's milk

● actual size

coral slime

● actual size

Several species of slime mold grow in the Greenbelt North Woods, and they are single-celled creatures that grow large enough that the single cell is visible to the naked eye. This category of slime mold is called the "Myxomycetes." These creatures push the limit of how large a living thing can grow while remaining a single cell. The cell contains multiple nuclei and has a reinforced cell wall called a peridium. Slime molds grow spores to reproduce.

dog vomit slime mold (*Fuligo septica*). This slime mold grows to be several inches across and can be yellow, orange, or off-white. It can withstand high concentrations of zinc without dying (Wikipedia, *Fuligo septica*).

wolf's milk (*Lycogala epidendrum*). This slime mold takes the form of spheres that are about 1/4–1/2 inch in diameter. The spheres form during summer and contain microscopic spores. At first, a sphere's color is pink, changing to brown as it matures.

coral slime (*Ceratiomyxa fruticulosa*). This slime mold forms its spores on the outside of white, finger-like structures that are so small that they are barely visible to the naked eye. The finger-like bodies can merge to form a spherical starburst or honeycomb structure approximately 1/8 inch across. Coral slime mold is of the most common slime molds in the world (https://www.messiah.edu/Ceratiomyxa%20fruticulosa.htm).

Above, greenshield lichen (top) and ruffle lichen (bottom). Below, ruffle lichen (left) and greenshield lichen (right).

dust lichen

whitewash lichen

flame lichen

217

script lichen

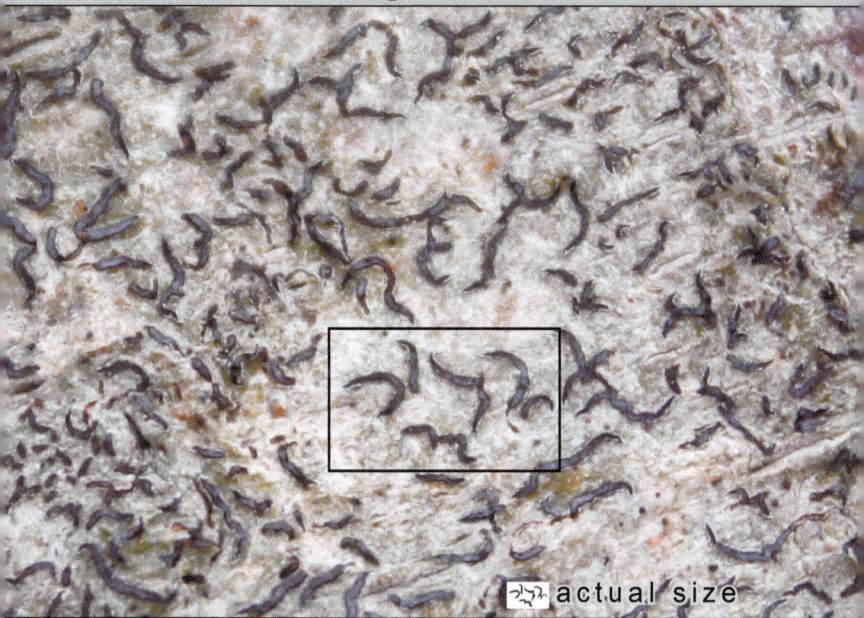

actual size

powderhorn lichen

A lichen is two living things in one. A lichen is a fungus that cannot live without the food produced by algae that the fungus cultivates within its own body.

Lichens in the Greenbelt North Woods grow almost exclusively on the bark of living or dead trees, whereas some lichen species in other forests grow on soil or rock. Whatever surface a lichen is growing on, it does not extract nutrients from that surface. Instead, it extracts nutrients to produce food from raindrops that fall on it and from the surrounding air. For this reason, lichens, like moss, are called epiphytic, a word whose etymology means a living thing (-phyte) living on the surface (epi-) of another living thing.

Lichens can take on a variety of growth forms that resemble either a wrinkly sheet of paper (folios), scattered dust (leprose), a mat of branches (fruticose), or patches of paint (crustose). When dry, lichens may be either pale green, gray, white, or yellow. When wet, lichens often turn bright green.

Lichens are sensitive to air pollution, so the range of lichen species that a trained biologist can spot in a forest may be used as an indicator of how clean the air is. Paint-like lichens are a sign of a more mature forest than are leafy or bushy lichens. Walewski (2007, pg. 92) states this fact using technical terms: "many crustose lichens are a sign of an older successional lichen community." For more information, see Brodo et al. (2001). The lichen photos in the preceding pages are magnified from 5× to 10× life-size, except for the photos of greenshield and ruffle lichens, which are close to life-size.

greenshield lichen (*Flavoparmelia*). One of the most common lichens in the Eastern US. This lichen has a leafy appearance, it is pale green, and it has a scalloped edge. At the center of a mature specimen, dull-colored grains are found, each less than a millimeter across. Such a grain is called a soredium (plural: soredia) and, it is one way for the lichen to spread. Each soredium contains algae surrounded by a fungus filament, i.e., a sample of all of the members of the fungus-algae community that is a lichen. The soredia break off when something brushes against the lichen. These grains are sometimes called "spores," but they are really complete bits of lichen that are capable of starting a new specimen wherever they land. The true spores of other fungus are much smaller, i.e., a single cell.

ruffle lichen (*Parmotrema*). This leafy lichen is gray, and its edge stands up from the bark. Ruffle lichen has black hairs along its edge that resemble a baby's eyelashes. These black hairs are only about 2 millimeters long (about the thickness of a penny). Ruffle lichen may be seen growing on the same branch as greenshield lichen. Ruffle lichen is widespread in the Eastern US.

dust lichen (*Lepraria*). This lichen is pastel green or bright green. It has a painted-on look and a granular texture.

whitewash lichen (*Phlyctis argena*). This lichen is white and smooth. Growing on tree bark, it has a painted-on look. The lichen may have white sand-like grains on it. SIMILAR SPECIES: If close inspection reveals scattered black disks 0.5 millimeter across, see rosette lichen (next page). If close inspection reveals black squiggly lines that resemble writing, see script lichen (next page).

flame lichen (*Candelaria*) or **sunburst lichen** (*Xanthoria*). At at distance, both of these lichens look like flat bright-yellow dots under 1/8 inch across.

Examination of these yellow dots with a strong magnifying glass will reveal that each dot is actually shaped somewhat like a glove with extremely thin fingers that are about 0.05 millimeter across.

rosette lichen (*Physcia*). Lichens in this genus are typically gray or pale green and grow in patches that are rarely over an inch across. The edge of a patch is finely ruffled. Sometimes the patch has, on top of it, a scattering of miniature mushroom-shaped bodies with black circular tops. These bodies are about 0.5 millimeters across and are called "apothecia." SIMILAR SPECIES: If the edge of the lichen is flat against bark with apothecia present, then it might be button lichen (*Buellia)*. See the discussion of *Physcia* in Brodo et al. (2001, pg. 546).

script lichen (*Graphis scripta*). Growing on tree bark, this lichen looks like a patch of thin white paint. Looking very closely at the white patch, one can see thin, meandering black lines that are sometimes branched. The black lines are the reproductive bodies of this lichen. The black lines are generally 1–3 millimeters long and 0.2–0.4 millimeters wide. In the Greenbelt North Woods, script lichen is often found on ironwood trunks in the Goddard Branch floodplain.

powderhorn lichen (*Cladonia coniocraea*). Mature examples of this lichen consist of both a bright-green leaf-like structure, a few millimeters across, and also tall cones that are pale pastel green, 1/2 inch tall, and very thin. Powderhorn lichens, like other lichens in this genus, are called two-part lichens because a leaf-like structure grows first and then a narrow, spiky structure grows.

Glossary

This book uses the following informal terms to describe the shapes of various plants. Example species and their page numbers are provided to illustrate most of these terms.

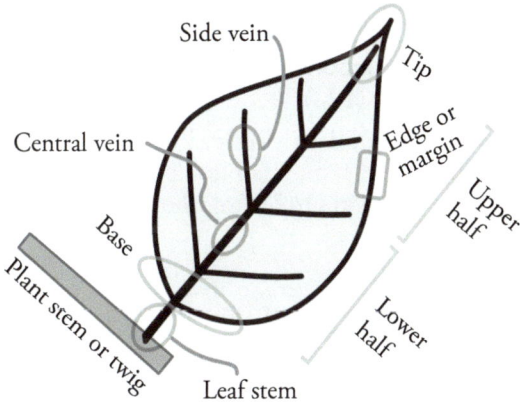

Leaf Shape

Oval: hickory (pg. 43), beech (58), black locust (46), chestnut oak (20).

Lobed: most oaks (17), red maple (33), tulip poplar (32), sweetgum (34), sycamore (34).

Spade shaped: redbud (68), common blue violet (166), garlic mustard (148), hairy bittercress (149).

Widest near tip: black gum (62), sweetpepperbush (102).

Widest near base: black walnut (44), pear (61), amur honeysuckle (88), strawberry bush (100), wintercreeper (101).

Uneven base: elm (59).

Leaf Side Veins

Parallel to each other: straight side veins are parallel to each other on each side of the leaf. chestnut oak (pg. 20), black walnut (44), beech (58), chinquapin (59), elm (59), ironwood (59).

Curved toward the tip: side veins curve toward the tip of the leaf. dogwood (63).

Radial: side veins originate from a point at the base of the leaf. sweetgum (34), sycamore (34), redbud (68), English ivy (122).

Parallel to the leaf edge: greenbrier (120), pink lady's slipper (131), cranefly orchid (147), Solomon's seal (156).

Leaf Arrangement

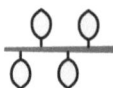

Alternate: most trees (pg. 7), Solomon's seal (156).

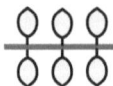

Opposite: many bushes (77), red maple (33), dogwood (63), vetch (171).

Whorled: more than two leaves coming from the same point. cleavers (158), Indian cucumber (158), wild yam (170).

Compound: more than one leaf coming from the same bud and sharing the same leaf stem. some trees (42), some bushes and vines (112).

Double compound: mimosa tree (44), devil's walking stick (112).

Leaf Edge

‾‾‾‾‾‾ **Smooth:** white oak (pg. 17), hickory (43), black locust (46), black gum (62), redbud (68), heath (86).

〰〰〰 **Fine toothed:** teeth are so small that they are hard to see at arm's length. cherry (60), pear (61), burning bush (100), strawberry bush (100), blackhaw viburnum (101).

∧∧∧∧ **Coarse toothed:** teeth are approx. 1/8 inch high. sycamore (34), beech (58), arrowwood viburnum (103), star-of-Bethlehem (163).

∧∧∧∧ **Double toothed:** fine teeth are super-imposed on coarse teeth. elm (59), ironwood (59).

〰〰 **Wavy:** edge of leaf is shaped like a snake crawling. chestnut oak (20), cottonwood (69).

⌒⌒⌒ **Rounded:** when describing clothing, this sort of edge is called "scalloped." garlic mustard (148), hairy bittercress (149).

Symbols

◀ ▶   An associated photo can be found on either a preceding or following page.

Invasive species: A species that is non-native to the mid-Atlantic region and that tends to crowd out native species and reduce biodiversity.

Flower Shape

Disk: ● small white aster (pg. 138); ✳ dove's foot cranesbill (138); ✳ star-of-Bethlehem (163); ❀ dogwood (63).

Rose-like: Five white petals in a disk. mayapple (131), wine raspberry (115), blackberry (114), multiflora rose (113), pear (61), cherry (60).

Bowl: tulip poplar (32), mountain laurel (85), barberry (85), lesser celandine (149).

Bell: smooth Solomons seal (156), speedwell (166), snowflake (162), blueberry (87), spring beauty (157).

Trumpet: partridge berry (87), red maple (33), columbine (138).

Inconspicuous petals: false Solomon seal (156), meadow rue (138), holly (62), Indian cucumber root (158), mimosa tree (44).

Pea-like: An upper "bonnet" petal, two side "wing" petals, and a tongue. black locust (46), redbud (68), vetch (171), wild yam (170), tick trefoil (139), wisteria (112).

Mint-like: Fused petals form an upper and lower "lip." purple dead nettle (166), bugleweed (167), archangel (157), creeping charlie (167), honeysuckle (89).

Seed-bearing Body

Nut meat   • Seed
Fleshy or dry   Shell or stem

Berry: a fleshy fruit containing seeds. black gum (pg. 62), blackhaw viburnum (101), blueberry (87), devil's walking stick (112), English ivy (122), greenbrier (120), mile-a-minute vine (170), Virginia creeper (113), Indian cucumber root (158), sassafras (33); arrowwood (99), barberry (85), bittersweet (102), dogwood (63), holly (62), honeysuckle (89), jack-in-the-pulpit (132), maple-leaved viburnum (120), multiflora rose (113), partridge berry (87), spicebush (87); mayapple (131); poison ivy (113).

Nut with fleshy husk: husks are pale green in summer and black when ripe in autumn. hickory (38), black walnut (44).

Nut with bur: a bur is a hard, brown covering with spikes. beech (58), chinquapin (59).

Seed ball: may consist entirely of seeds as in sycamore (34), or may consist of hard, tan material that releases seeds: sweetgum (62).

Acorn: oak (17).

Cone: pine (72).

Pod: a pea-like seed container. black locust (46), redbud (68), tick trefoil (139), vetch (171), wild yam (170), wisteria (112).

Samara: a seed with a wing. tulip poplar (32), red maple (33), elm (59), box elder (44), tree of heaven (46).

Capsule: A dry container that splits open to release seeds. *with arms*: columbine (138), azalea (86), orchids (147, 131); *spherical*: mountain laurel (85), sweetpep-perbush (102).

227

Growth Form

As a first step to determining the species of an unfamiliar plant, a botanist may first categorize the plant's general appearance, a basic approach that inspired the organization of this field guide. A plant's overall shape is called its "growth form" or "habit." A plant may also be categorized by whether or not its stem has wood and bark. If so, it is a woody plant, otherwise an herbaceous plant. The following informal terms are used in this field guide to group plants into categories, and only some of these terms have a precise scientific meaning.

Tree: A woody plant with one main stem at the ground.

Bush: A woody plant with multiple stems at the ground.

Central stem: An herbaceous plant with its main stem upright and unbranched.

Bushy: An herbaceous plant with its main stem upright and branched.

Grass-like: An herbaceous plant with a tuft of long, narrow, upright leaves emerging from the ground.

Basal rosette: An herbaceous plant with a whorl of leaves flat on the ground and a separate, upright flower stem.

Climbing vine: A plant that climbs a supporting object if it encounters one.

Ground cover: A plant that stays within a few inches of the ground and that may be, but is not necessarily, a vine.

References

Abrams, M. D., 1998: The red maple paradox: what explains the widespread expansion of red maple in eastern forests? *BioScience*, **48**, 355–364.

Abrams, M. D., 2000: Fire and the ecological history of oak forests in the Eastern US. Proceedings paper GTR-NE-274, *Workshop on Fire, People, and the Central Hardwoods Landscape*.

Abrams, M. D., 2003: Where has all the white oak gone? *BioScience*, **53**, 927–939.

Abrams, M,. D., 2007: Tales from the blackgum, a consummate subordinate tree. *BioScience,* **57**, 347–359.

Besley, F. W., 1913: *The Forests of Prince George's County*. MD Board of Forestry, 41 pp.

Brodo, I. M., S. D. Sharnoff, and S. Sharnoff, 2001: *Lichens of North American*. Yale Univ. Press, 795 pp.

Burns, R., M., and B. H. Honkala, 1990: *Silvics of North America*. USDA Forest Service, Agricultural Handbook #654, 877 pp. Available online at https://www.srs.fs.usda.gov/pubs/misc/ag_654/table_of_contents.htm.

Choukas-Bradley M., 2004: *Eastern Woodland Wildflowers & Trees: 350 Plants Observed at Sugarloaf Mountain, Maryland*. Univ. Virginia Press, 415 pp.

Choukas-Bradley, M., 2008: *City of Trees: The Complete Field Guide to the Trees of Washington, D.C.* 3rd ed., Univ. VA Press, 438 pp.

Cohen, R., 1985 June 12: Memorandum on Natural Areas. "Buffer behind house" folder in box 1 of special collection 2006-117-MDHC, University of Maryland library, College Park. Quote from pg. 3: "Comment on comments heard

recently: Brambles are 'messy,' and poison ivy should be eradicated everywhere it grows. What these observations suggest
is that people sometimes forget that the woods exact respect
from those who visit them. Protective clothing and awareness
of the shape of unfriendly ivies are the answer for this unusual
community of people and native wildlife, not a machete."

DNR, 2019: *Rare, Threatened, and Endangered Plants of
Maryland.* expanded version, Maryland Dept. Natural
Resources, March 2019, 224 pp. Available online at https://
dnr.maryland.gov/wildlife/Documents/rte_Plant_List_
expanded.pdf. County-specific endangered species lists are
available, including one for Prince George's County: https://
dnr.maryland.gov/wildlife/Pages/plants_wildlife/rte/rteplants.
aspx.

eFloras, 2019: *Flora of North America North of Mexico.* Flora
of North America Editorial Committee, eds. Published on
the Internet at http://www.efloras.org. A less technical survey
focused on Maryland plants is provided by the Maryland
Biodiversity Project at https://www.marylandbiodiversity.
com. Plant identification assistance was obtained from both
the "Plant Identification" and "Greenbelt Biota" groups on
https://www.facebook.com.

Griffith, L. D., 2008: *Flowers and Herbs of Early America.* Yale
Univ. Press, 292 pp.

Higgins, A., 5 April 2017: The dogwood tree—the living symbol
of the American spring—makes a comeback. *Washington Post.*
Available online at https://www.washingtonpost.com/.

Hilgedick, K., 2017 October: Bountiful, beneficial black
walnuts. *Missouri Conservationist*, **78**, 22–27.

Hotchkiss, N., 1940: *Flora of the Patuxent Research Refuge,
Maryland.* Wildlife Leaflet BS-154, US Dept. Interior,
Bureau of Biological Survey. Available online at http://www.
biodiversitylibrary.org/item/135558#page/3/mode/1up.

Hotchkiss, N., and R. E. Stewart, 1979: *Vegetation and
Vertebrates of the Patuxent Wildlife Research Center: Outline
of Ecology and Annotated Lists.* 65 pp. Available online at
https://ecos.fws.gov/ServCat/DownloadFile/45841?Ref-
erence=44971.

Hartzler, B., 2019: Multiflora rose and rose rosette disease. Iowa
State Univ., Extension and Outreach. Available online at

https://crops.extension.iastate.edu/multiflora-rose-and-rose-rosette-disease.

Kartesz, J. T., 2015: The Biota of North America Program (BONAP), online atlas, Chapel Hill, NC. County-level species range maps published online at http://bonap.net/.

Knapp, W. M., and R. Wiegand, 2014: Orchid (Orchidaceae) decline in the Catoctin Mountains, Frederick County, Maryland as documented by a long-term dataset. *Biodiversity Conservation*, **23**, 1965–1976. Discusses overgrazing by deer on orchids.

MacKay, B., 2013: *A Year Across Maryland*. John Hopkins Univ. Press, 300 pp.

Martin, L. C., 1989: *Southern Wildflowers*. Longstreet Press, 272 pp.

McKnight, K. B., J. R. Rohrer, K. M. Ward, and W. J. Perdrizet, 2013: *Common Mosses of the Northeast and Appalachians*. Princeton Univ. Press, 391 pp.

Moore, A, 2017: *Pawpaw: In Search of America's Forgotten Fruit*. Chelsea Green Publishing, 320 pp.

MD State Archives, 2019: Maryland at a glance: state symbols. Web page. https://msa.maryland.gov/msa/mdmanual/01glance/symbols/html/tree.html.

Phillips, R., 2005: *Mushrooms and Other Fungus of North America*. Firefly Books, 319 pp.

Peattie, D. C., 1948: *A Natural History of Trees of Eastern and Central North America*. Houghton Mifflin Harcourt, 606 pp.

Pulice, C. E., and A. A. Packer, 2008: Simulated herbivory induces extrafloral nectary production in *Prunus avium*. *Functional Ecology*, **22**, 801–807, doi: 10.1111/j.1365-2435.2008.01440.x.

Russell, B., 2006: *Field Guide to Wild Mushrooms of Pennsylvania and the Mid-Atlantic*. Penn. State Univ. Press, 236 pp.

Sanders, J., 2003: *The Secrets of Wildflowers*. Globe Pequot Press, 304 pp.

Stein, J., D. Binion, and R. Acciavatti, 2003: *Field Guide to Native Oak Species of Eastern North America*. USDA, FHTET-2003-01. Available online at https://www.fs.fed.us/foresthealth/technology/pdfs/fieldguide.pdf.

Sullivan, J., 1994: *Cercis canadensis* in Fire Effects Information System, USDA Forest Service. Available online at https://www.fs.fed.us/database/feis/plants/tree/cercan/all.html.

Swearingen, J., B. Slattery, K. Reshetiloff, and S. Zwicker, 2010: *Plant invaders of Mid-Altlantic Natural Areas*. 4th ed., National Park Service, 168 pp. Was formerly available at https://www.nps.gov/plants/ALIEn/pubs/midatlantic/. The author now works at https://in-the-weeds.com/. See also the University of Georgia's online Invasive Plant Atlas of the US: https://www.invasiveplantatlas.org/subject.html?sub=3024.

Terrell, E. E., and coauthors, 2000: *Annotated List of the Flora of the Beltsville Agricultural Research Center, Beltsville, Maryland*. ARS-155, USDA, 89 pp. Available online at https://www.biodiversitylibrary.org/item/233329#page/3/mode/1up.

Thieret, J. W., 2001: *National Audubon Society Field Guide to North American Wildflowers, Eastern Region*. Alfred A. Knopf, 879 pp.

Walewski, J., 2007: *Lichens of the North Woods: A field guide to 111 northern lichens*. Kollath+Stensaas Publishing, 152 pp.

Wikipedia, 2019: Wikipedia: The Free Encyclopedia. Website, https://en.wikipedia.org/wiki/Main_Page.

Willis, K., and J. McElwain, 2014: *The Evolution of Plants*. 2nd ed., Oxford Univ. Press, 425 pp.

Yun, H. Y., 2019: Multiflora rose rust - *Phragmidium rosae-multiflorae*. Systematic Mycology and Microbiology Laboratory - Invasive Fungi Fact Sheets, USDA Agricultural Research Service. Available online at https://nt.ars-grin.gov/taxadescriptions/factsheets/index.cfm?thisapp=Phragmidium-rosae-multiflorae.

Index

flame lichen, 221

flowering season start
February
  skunk cabbage, 131
March
  forsythia, 102
  red maple, 33
April
  Ajuga reptans, 167
  archangel, yellow, 157
  blackberry, 114
  blueberry, 87
  celandine, lesser 149
  columbine, 138
  dove's foot cranesbill, 138
  garlic mustard, 148
  ground ivy, 167
  hairy bittercress, 149
  jack-in-the-pulpit, 132
  mayapple, 131
  mock strawberry, 170
  periwinkle, 88
  pink lady's slipper, 131
  pinkster azalea, 86
  purple dead nettle, 166
  speedwell, 166
  spicebush, 87
  spring beauty, 157
  star-of-Bethlehem, 163
  viburnum,101, 120
  violet, 166
May
  honeysuckle, 89
  Indian cucumber root, 158
  mountain laurel, 85
  multiflora rose, 113
  partridge berry, 87
  snowflake, 162

Solomon's seal, 156
strawberry bush, 100
tulip poplar, 32
June
  heal-all, 167
  meadow rue, 138
August
  burdock, 149
  sweetpepperbush, 102
  tick trefoil, 139
  wisteria, 112
September
  small white aster, 138

fruit of woody plants
acorn, 17
blue, purple, black
  blackberry, 114
  black gum, 62
  blackhaw viburnum, 101
  blueberry, 87
  devil's walking stick, 112
  English ivy, 122
  greenbrier, 120
  mile-a-minute, 170
  Virginia creeper, 113
brown, seed pod
  forsythia, 102
  mountain laurel, 85
  periwinkle, 88
  pinkster azalea, 86
cone, 75
fleshy black: skunk cabbage, 131
green: callery pear, 61
nut with husk
  beech, 58
  chinquapin, 59
  hickory, 42
  ironwood, 59

Additional Species

This field guide is intended as an introduction, and therefore, it does not picture every species growing in the Greenbelt North Woods. The following is a partial list of species that are not pictured in this book but that local naturalists have reported finding in the North Woods. **Trees:** blackjack oak (*Quercus marilandica*), post oak (*Q. stellata*), swamp white oak (*Q. bicolor*), poison sumac (*Toxicodendron vernix*), and red cedar (*Juniperus virginiana*). **Other woody plants:** swamp azalea (*Rhododendron viscosum*), striped wintergreen (*Chimaphila maculata*), and dewberry (*Rubus*). **Herbaceous plants:** green wood orchid (*Platanthera clavellata*), large whorled pogonia (*Isotria verticillata*), white wood aster (*Aster divaricatus*), golden rod (*Solidago*), squawroot (*Conopholis americana*), beech drops (*Epifagus virginiana*), lady fern (*Athyrium*), royal fern (*Osmunda spectabilis*), and maidenhair fern (*Adiantum*). **Fungi:** chicken of the woods (*Laetiporus*).

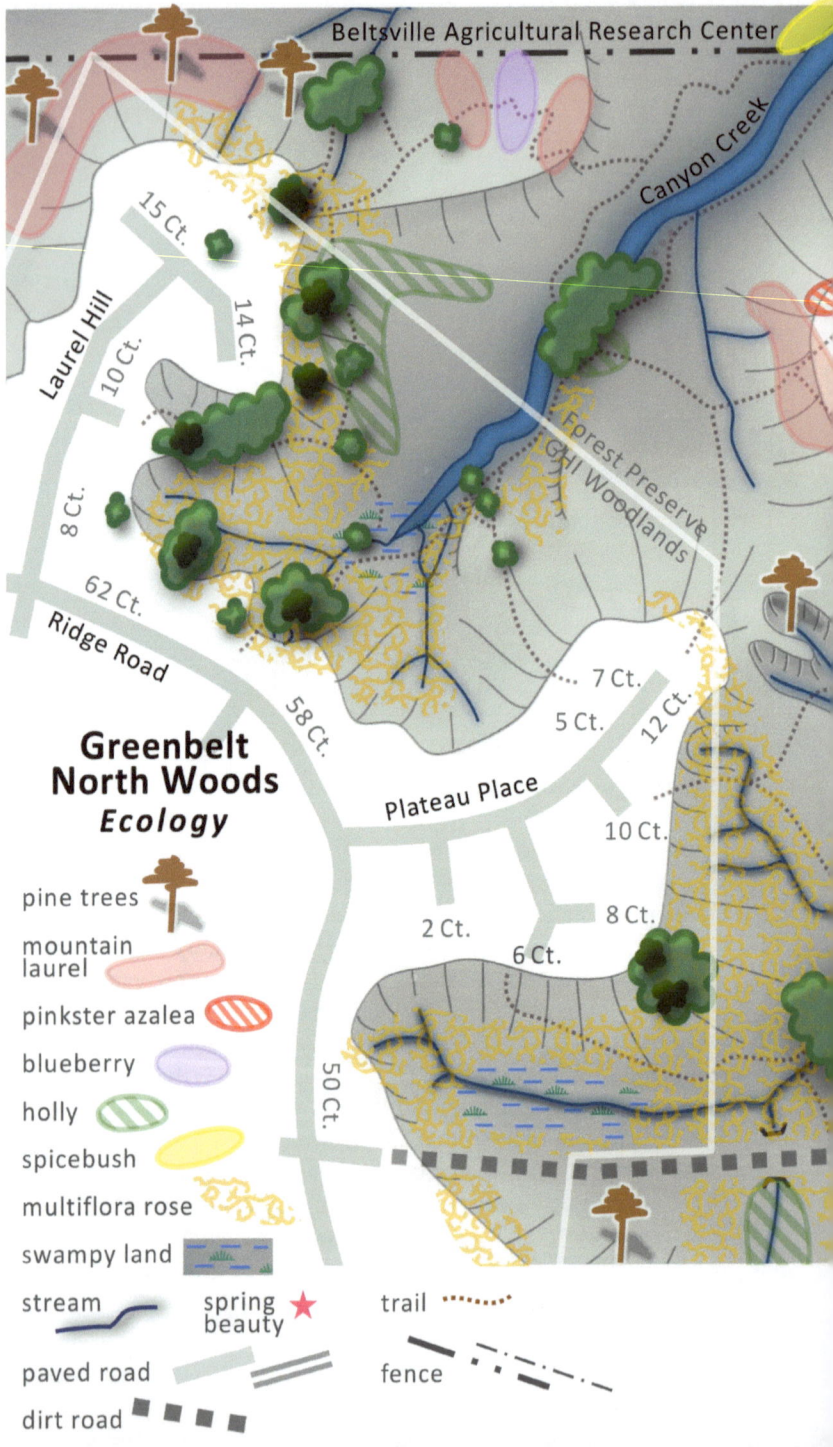

Beltsville Agricultural Research Center

Canyon Creek

15 Ct.

14 Ct.

Laurel Hill

10 Ct.

8 Ct.

62 Ct.

Ridge Road

58 Ct.

Forest Preserve
GHI Woodlands

7 Ct.

5 Ct.

12 Ct.

10 Ct.

Plateau Place

8 Ct.

2 Ct.

6 Ct.

50 Ct.

Greenbelt
North Woods
Ecology

pine trees	
mountain laurel	
pinkster azalea	
blueberry	
holly	
spicebush	
multiflora rose	
swampy land	

stream   spring beauty ★   trail ......

paved road    fence

dirt road

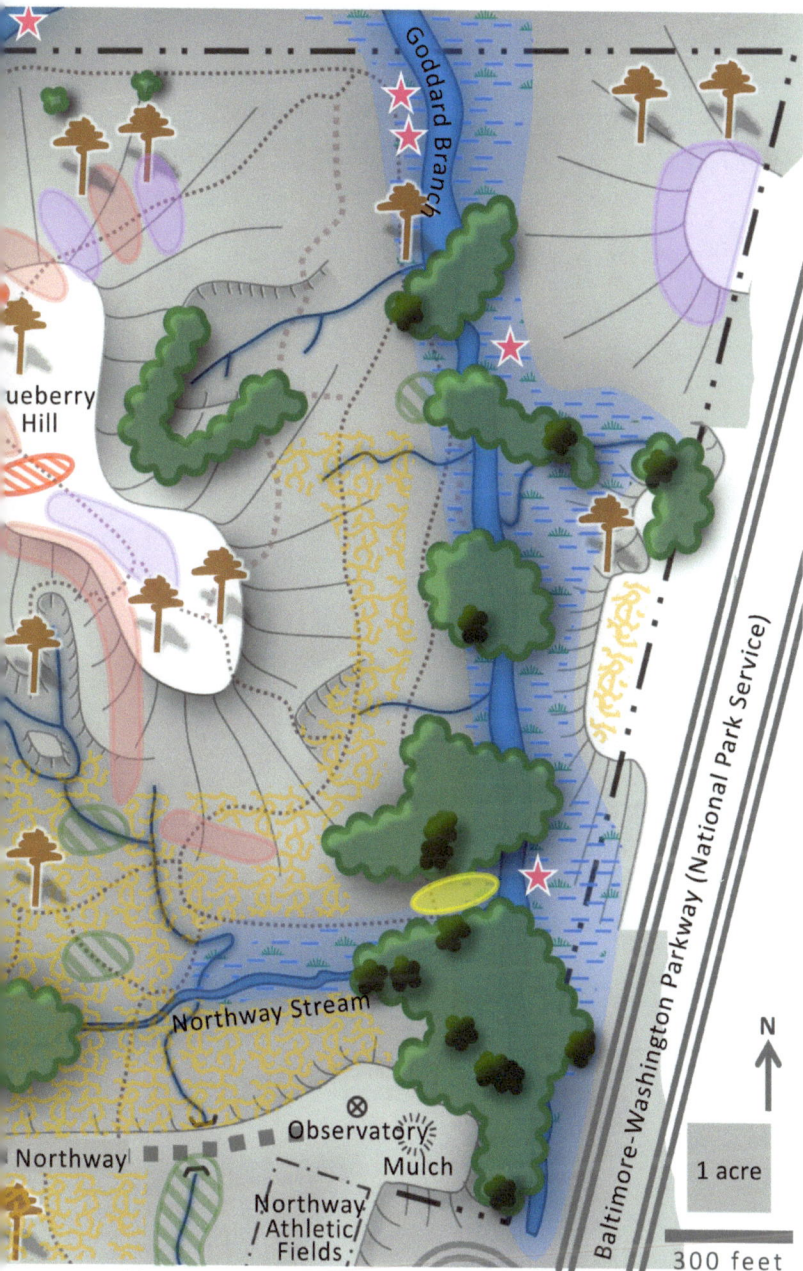

Old trees, meaning that a number of trees have trunks at least 30 inches in diameter at chest height.

One or more oak or maple with a 36-inch-diameter trunk or a tulip poplar with a 42-inch-diameter trunk.

Beltsville Agricultural Research Center

Canyon Creek

Laurel Hill

Ridge Road

Plateau Place

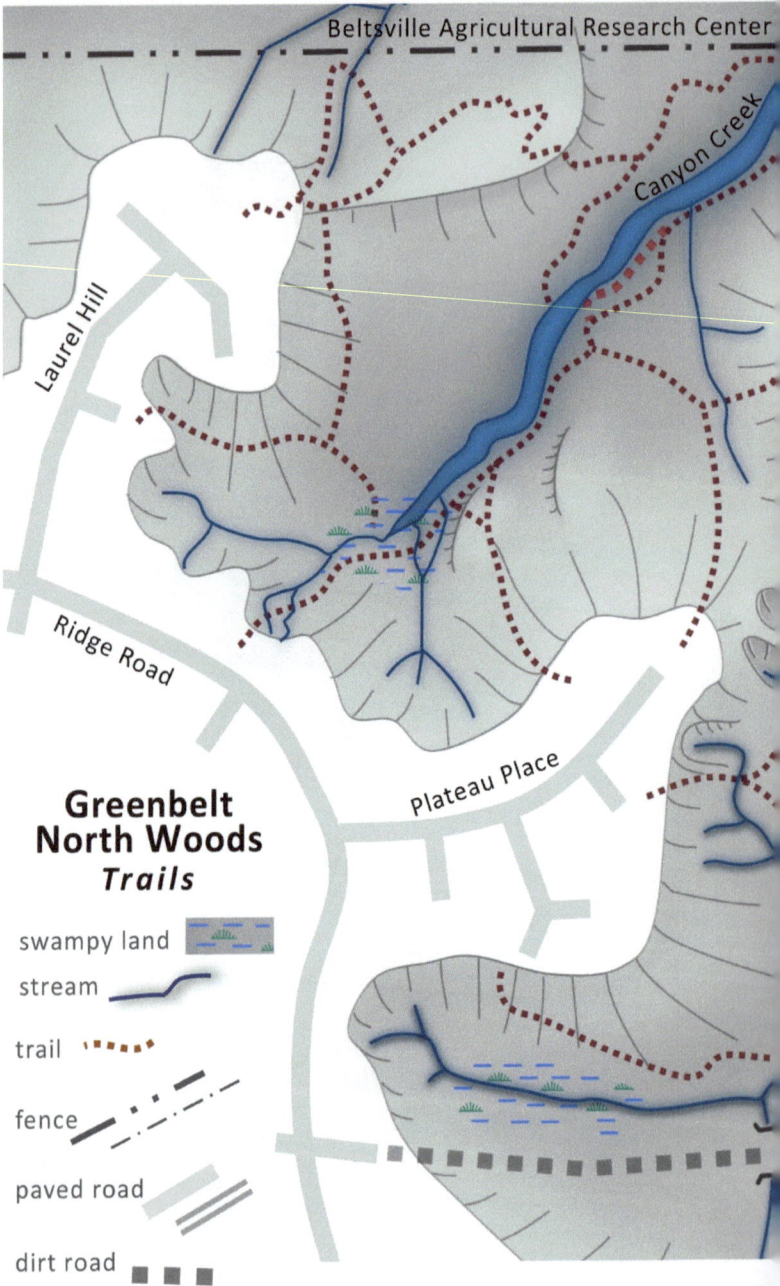

Greenbelt
North Woods
Trails

swampy land

stream

trail

fence

paved road

dirt road

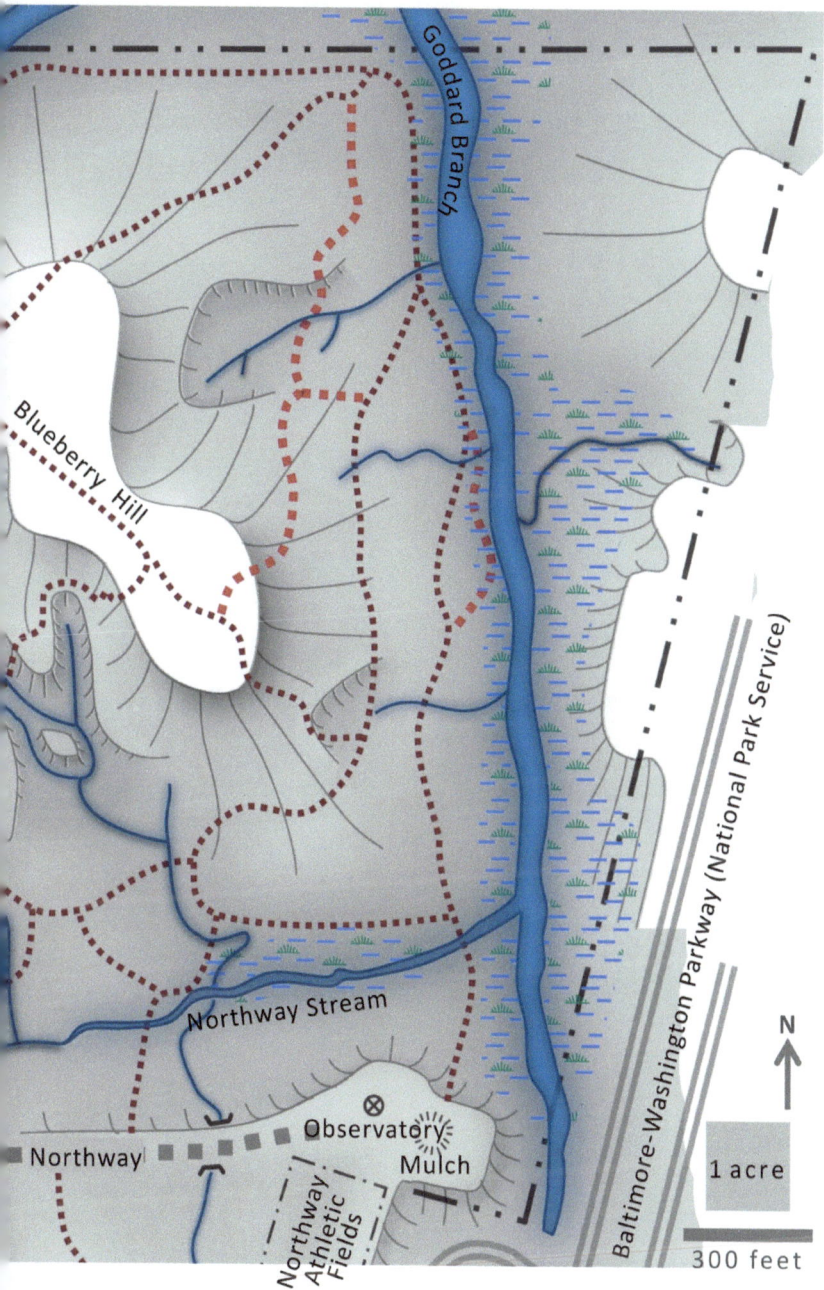

Goddard Branch

Blueberry Hill

Baltimore-Washington Parkway (National Park Service)

Northway Stream

Observatory

Northway

Mulch

Northway Athletic Fields

N

1 acre

300 feet

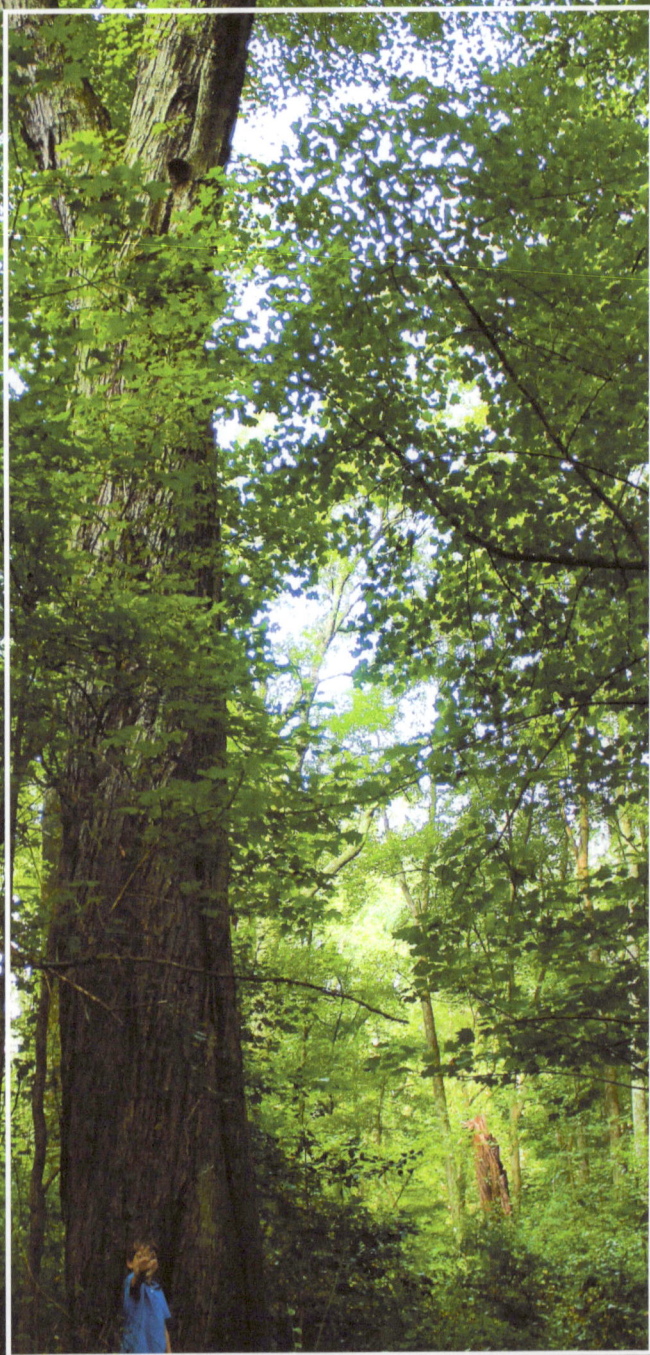

------- Book ordering ---

A Hundred Wild Things: A Field Guide to Plants in the Greenbelt North Woods by Owen A. Kelley ©2019, ISBN 978-0-9670633-3-1

To order a copy from the author, send an email to okelley@gmu.edu or mail a check for $25.00 ($23.58 per book plus 6% Maryland sales tax) to the following address:

  Owen A. Kelley
  15 Lakeside Drive
  Greenbelt, MD 20770

www.ingramcontent.com/pod-product-compliance
Lightning Source LLC
Chambersburg PA
CBHW040931030426
42334CB00007B/108